THE CIVIL WAR HISTORY SERIES

PIEDMONT SOLDIERS AND THEIR FAMILIES

LT. JAMES B. WASHINGTON was photographed by James F. Gibson on May 31, 1862, with Capt. George A. Custer of the 5th Cavalry in Fair Oaks, Virginia. (LOC.)

COVER: PLEASANT HENDERSON HANES (OCTOBER 16, 1845–JUNE 9, 1925) was born to Alexander Martin and Jane March Hanes. He is shown here with his grandchildren—Jarvis Aubrey is on his lap, and the others are, from left to right, Newton, Huber Jr., Rosalie, Tol Old, and William Marvin. Please see pp. 41–42 for further information. (HH.)

THE CIVIL WAR HISTORY SERIES

PIEDMONT SOLDIERS AND THEIR FAMILIES

CINDY H. CASEY

TEMPUS

Published by Arcadia Publishing,
an imprint of Tempus Publishing, Inc.
2 Cumberland Street
Charleston, SC 29401

Printed in Great Britain.

Library of Congress Catalog Card Number: 00-102886

For all general information contact Arcadia Publishing at:
Telephone 843-853-2070
Fax 843-853-0044
E-Mail sales@arcadiapublishing.com

For customer service and orders:
Toll-Free 1-888-313-2665

Visit us on the internet at http://www.arcadiaimages.com

A CONFEDERATE GUN EMPLACEMENT above Dutch Gap, near James River, Virginia, was photographed in 1865.

CONTENTS

Acknowledgments   6

Introduction   7

Credits   8

1. Tenth Ohio Cavalry: No Pillaging Allowed!   9

2. Winston and Salem: Home Fires Burning   17

3. Call out the Militia: Protecting the Home Front   31

4. From Plow-Boys to Soldiers: The Sacrifice of Life or Limb   43

5. Twenty-Sixth Regiment, NC Troops: A Home for Salem's Band   79

6. Twenty-First Regiment, NC Troops: Remembering Our Men   89

7. Battlefields and Prisons: Their Spirits Call to Us   115

THE ORIGINAL "DICTATOR" is shown here in Petersburg, Virginia, in an October 1864 photograph taken by David Knox. Its current whereabouts are unknown; lacking the real thing, Petersburg National Battlefield Superintendent J. Walter Coleman decided to duplicate the huge weapon out of concrete. Under the supervision of Park Historian Manning Voorhis, and through the labor force of the CCC, a facsimile of the weapon was built in 1935 and placed on the site where the original stood. (LOC.)

ACKNOWLEDGMENTS

I would like to thank those of you who unselfishly shared your photographs and family histories with me. Your generosity has placed your ancestors in a seat of honor, forever to be remembered in this special collection of images documenting their lives. I would like to give special thanks to Mr. Henry Yarbrough, who provided me with much wonderful local history and military information. Words cannot express my appreciation to Jerry, Bratis, and Tim, the wonderful guys of the NC Room who kept me stocked in research books! Special acknowledgment is made to the James B. Gordon United Daughters of the Confederacy. For over 100 years this chapter has supported Forsyth County through their memorial, patriotic, benevolent, educational, and historical services. Without their dedication to the preservation of books, documents, diaries, letters, and personal records of the Civil War era, much of our county's history would be lost. To my faithful friends, Judy Cardwell, Faye Jarvis Moran, and Mel White, a special thank you for your continual support. And finally, I want to thank my loving husband, Tom, for his boundless patience and love, which keeps me positive and on track! I Love You!!

WOUNDED FROM THE BATTLE OF THE WILDERNESS, May 5–7, 1864, were photographed in Fredericksburg by James B. Gardner. Of the 162,920 forces engaged in this battle, only 61,025 were Confederate. The CSA realized 11,400 casualties. Other names for this battle are Combats at Parker's Store, Craig's Meeting House, Todd's Tavern, Brock Road, and the Furnaces. (LOC.)

INTRODUCTION

North Carolina had not wanted to secede from the Union until President Lincoln called for troops from the Old North State. Choosing instead to support the Confederate cause, North Carolina furnished over 125,000 men, practically the state's entire adult white male population. More than 40,000 of these men lost their lives in the bloodiest war in American history. It has been written that even though North Carolina had about one-ninth of the population of the Confederacy, it furnished about one-seventh of the soldiers. One-sixth of the soldiers who surrendered with Lee at Appomattox were from North Carolina. Statistics are very important in historical research, but I believe that learning about the individuals who participated in this war is of equal importance.

My purpose for writing *Piedmont Soldiers and Their Families* was to acknowledge many of those long-forgotten soldiers and the families whose contributions and sacrifices were instrumental in the transformation of our nation. I hope these biographies will provide a fresh prospective to the Civil War, and a renewed respect for those who have passed before us.

Author's Note: Sources of information and images are abbreviated in the text as follows: Allen Snow (AS); Annie M.V. Russell, *The Schaubs and Vests of North Carolina* (AMVR); Becky Lassiter (BL); Bert M. Vogler (BMV); Charles M. Vogler, Chairman of Documentation Committee, Philip Christoph Vogler Memorial, Inc., *Descendants of Philip Christoph Vogler* (PCVM); Collection of Old Salem, Inc. (COS); *Confederate Veteran* magazine (CVM); Elizabeth Tesh Burke (ETB); Faye Jarvis Moran (FJM); Frank B. Hanes Sr., (FBH); Frank Graham Moss (FGM); Hamilton Horton (HH); Harold and Elizabeth Vogler (HEV); Henry Yarbrough (HY); Hester Bartlett Jackson, *Surry County Soldiers in the Civil War* (HBJ); Homer Snow (HS); Jean Darnell Bolt (JDB); Jessie S. Barbour (JSB); Jim Cockerham (JC); Jo Beth Boyles (JBB); Joann Combs Self (JCS); John T. McGee (JTM); John T. Spach (JTS); Judy S. Cardwell (JSC); Keith Redmon (KR); Lawrence Alspaugh, M.D. (LA); Library of Congress (LOC); Louis Shaffner, M.D. (LS); Mildred Ann Transou Nicholson Flint (MATNF); Moravian Music Foundation (MMF); Mr. and Mrs. Fred Hill (FH); Mr. and Mrs. Troy Church (TC); Mrs. Hamilton Bolling (MHB); NC Room, Forsyth County Library (NCR); Nancy R. Petree (NRP); North Carolina Archives (NCA); Oren Palmer (OP); Patricia S. Beeson (PSB); Peggy J. Tesh (PJT); *Peoples Press*, May 15, 1863 (PP); Phyllis Roberson Hoots (PRH); Roger Horton (RH); Sam Spach Dalton (SSD); Sandra Butner Ray (SBR); Sandra C. Turney (SCT); Shirley Tuttle (ST); Southern Historical Collection, UNC, Chapel Hill (SHC); Stacy C. Slater (SCS); Steve Covington (SC); Teresa Lee Stout Stevens (TLSS); Thomas S. Boyles (TSB); Thomas H. Rothrock Sr., *Philip Jacob Rothrock 1713–1803* (THR); and Wilma Hiatt (WH) The primary sources used for military research were as follows: *North Carolina Troops 1861–1865* by Weymouth T. Jordon Jr. and Louis H. Manarin; *Twenty-Sixth NC State Troops, CSA* by Jeffery Weaver; *History of North Carolina*, by R.D.W. Connor; *North Carolina Regiment 1861–1865*, by Walter Clark; as well as selected personal diaries and autobiographies of that era.

THE BATTLE OF SPOTSYLVANIA COURT HOUSE took place on May 8–21, 1864. Of the 152,000 forces engaged, only 52,000 were Confederates. Despite this, the Union suffered 18,000 casualties to the Confederates 12,000. Timothy H. O'Sullivan took this view from the Beverly House looking toward Spotsylvania Court House, Virginia, on May 19, 1864. (LOC.)

One

TENTH OHIO CALVARY:
NO PILLAGING ALLOWED

THE WEST SIDE OF MAIN STREET, SALEM, is shown here *c.* 1866. A.B. Chaffin's Salem Hotel (the original tavern dining rooms) is located on the left. Many young men gathered here to volunteer with the 11th NC Volunteers. From the hotel, up Main Street and toward Winston, the houses are as follows: the Blum house (1815), shoemaker Samuel Shulz's house (1819), gunsmith Christoph Vogler's house (1797), and the John Vogler house (1819). It was this thoroughfare that Colonel Palmer, his field and staff, and the 10th Ohio Cavalry traveled upon when they officially occupied the township of Salem on April 10, 1865. It was reported that, "with the exception of the clatter of the hoofs of the horses as they filed down Main Street, no one would have been able to realize that a body of 3,000 troops were passing through." Colonel Palmer and his Union troops were peacefully greeted by Rev. Robert De Schweinitz, principal of the Female Academy; Joshua Boner, Esq., mayor of Salem; T.J. Wilson, mayor of Winston; R.L. Patterson, Esq.; and John Blackburn, clerk of court. Blackburn noted in Forsyth's court records that: "The colonel went to the bank and placed a guard there. He then proceeded to the dwelling house of Joshua Boner, Esq. and made his headquarters there and his men encamped on the opposite side of the Creek near the Bridge, under the Stars and Stripes of the United States of America which had not been publicly exhibited for perhaps nearly four years." (COS.)

ABOVE: THE F. & H. FRIES COMPANY (C. 1840) consisted of a woolen mill, cotton mill, and a smoke house. The Fries' slaves, as well as hired hands, worked day and night to weave the gray cloth needed for uniforms, as well as making heavy denim jeans. (NCR.)

OPPOSITE, ABOVE: KREEMERS PREPARATORY SCHOOL is shown here between 1863 and 1868. Before 1860, the Forsyth County public school system had been established by Calvin H. Wiley. The first public schoolhouse in Winston was located on the northwest corner of Liberty and First, on a lot that had been deeded by the Moravians to the Forsyth County Commissions in 1849. The one-room structure housed students of all ages and was one of the first public buildings in the new town of Winston. One of the first teachers hired was Mrs. Eliza W. Kreemer, whose term was served during the Civil War years. During these turbulent times, efforts were made to transfer school funds to military purposes, but Mr. Wiley successfully resisted all attempts. It was his belief that the continuation of education in the community was vital for both children and adults. Disabled soldiers unable to return to their regiment often turned to teaching as an occupation. In the late 1800s, the school was torn down and replaced with the Brown and Williamson Tobacco Company. (NCR.)

OPPOSITE, BELOW: THE VIERLING HOUSE AND BARN (LOT 7 AND 8) are shown here in a c. 1860 ambrotype. In 1800, Dr. Samuel Benjamin Vierling received permission from the Moravian brethren to build his home on lot number 7 in the township of Salem. It is said this was the first brick residence erected. In 1853, the house was owned by Bishop Emil A. de Schweinitz. It became a center of much of the social life of Salem. His daughters came to be the wives of well-established men of the community: Adelaide was the first wife of Dr. Henry Bahnson; Agnes married John W. Fries; Leanor married Dr. N.S. Siewers; Emily married W.A. Lemly; and Anna married F.H. Fries. No doubt, many times during the war the ladies of sewing and knitting circles met here, sharing news of their beaus and husbands who were miles away. In May 1865, when Colonel Palmer's Union Army arrived at the townships of Salem and Winston, the Vierling house and its barns were immediately occupied. Almost 200 years later, the Vierling house is still providing comfort to its residents. (COS.)

UPON FORSYTH COUNTY'S FORMATION IN 1849, a new county government was established. Francis Fries designed the courthouse in the Greek Revival style. Its porch was 12 feet wide, and the Doric columns were 30 feet tall. The structure was made of red brick, measuring 44 by 60 feet. The courtroom was located on the second floor, with the ground floor being divided into six offices for governmental officials. The courthouse served as a part-time church for many denominations, as Winston's first civic center, and it housed political meetings and other public celebrations. (NCR.)

LEFT: AROUND 1772, THE GIRLS SCHOOL, the forerunner of the Salem Academy and College, began with only three students. As the years passed, more families settled in Salem and the school's membership grew. Seeing the need for expansion, the Moravians formally established the Girls Boarding School on October 31, 1802. By 1805, another expansion was needed. More buildings were built on what was developing into a formal campus. By 1854, there were 329 students attending the Girls Boarding School, which came to be known as Salem Academy. In 1856, the academy's Main Hall was completed, housing all the classrooms, dormitory rooms, the infirmary, and storage rooms. During the Civil War, the academy sheltered more than 200 ladies. Although many of the students were there before the war, families from all over began sending their daughters to the academy for refuge from the impending hostilities. Soon, the academy buildings along the square overflowed with students. Many of the girls were taken into private homes. The scarcity of food required the principal, Reverend De Schweinitz, to ride out through the countryside searching for supplies. (COS.)

RIGHT: FIRST METHODIST CHURCH, on Liberty Street, was built in 1854. Upon the completion of the church building, Reverend C.F. Deems preached the sermon of dedication to an overflowing congregation. No one could have guessed that 11 years hence Union forces would occupy their quiet church and community. It has been documented that, during the 10th Ohio Volunteer Cavalry's occupation of Salem (April through June 1865), Federal troops fraternized with the citizens, attended church, and at times were hospitably received into many homes. Their regimental chaplain at one time addressed the Salem Home Sunday School class and also addressed the emancipated slaves at St. Philip's Church, encouraging them "to settle down and become honest and industrious citizens." It is likely that soldiers, both Federal and Confederate, attended this church. (NCR.)

ABOVE: THIS SALEM ACADEMY PHOTOGRAPH dates from c. 1865. In 1772, when the Moravians opened a "school for little girls" in the Gemein Haus on the village square, they became pioneers in women's education in colonial America. During the "Intellectual Awakening" of the 1800s, women were no longer satisfied with the education of "household arts." There was a shift in public views as to the curriculum presently being offered. Realizing a need for more colleges, other religious denominations started building their own schools. The Chowan Baptist Female Institute was established at Murfreesboro in 1848. Oxford Female College was sponsored by the Baptists in 1851. The Methodists founded Greensboro Female College in 1838, and Davenport Female College at Lenoir in 1858. Statesville Female College and Peace Female Institute at Raleigh were founded by the Presbyterians in 1856 and 1857, respectively. (COS.)

OPPOSITE, ABOVE: THE C. 1785 SALEM SINGLE SISTER HOUSE is shown here c. 1882. The Moravian religion was made up of the choir (chor) system. Age, sex, or marital status determined whether you were placed in the Single Brothers, Single Sisters, Married People, Widows, Older Boys, Little Boys, Older Girls, or Little Girls choir. To prepare the young females of the community for marriage, the girls would enter the Single Sisters House, where they were taught the art of spinning, weaving, and housekeeping. Marriages were normally arranged by the church. There is no doubt that when the Union troops arrived in Salem, the Moravians were very protective of the ladies of the Single Sisters House. (COS.)

OPPOSITE, BELOW: THE MORAVIAN HOME CHURCH, the Boys School, and the Inspector's House are shown here from the west in a pre-1871 photograph. The original Boys School was organized in Salem. Their initial classes were held in the home of master carpenter Christian Triebel. In 1774, the Boys School was moved to the Single Brothers House. To accommodate the increasing population of students, a new Boys School was built in 1794. In 1810, at a cost of $4,850, the Inspector's House was built. The Moravian Home Church still has an active and dedicated membership. These buildings are the same ones the 10th Ohio Cavalry took temporary possession of at the close of the Civil War. They are now owned by Old Salem, Inc. (COS.)

VARIOUS BUILDINGS USED BY THE CONGREGATION OF ST. PHILIP'S CHURCH are shown here. The first structure is Dr. Shuman's original plantation house. In 1836, Dr. Shuman freed his slaves specifically to emigrate to Liberia. Before their departure, a Love Feast was held in the log church. The plantation site became what is now known as the Happy Hill community. The second building is the original 1823 log church after it had been covered with clapboard. The third structure is the 1861 brick St. Philip's Moravian, which was built to replace the original log church. In May 1865, the chaplain of the 10th Ohio Regiment stood at the podium of this church announcing to the congregation their freedom.

The institution of slavery in Salem dates back to mid-1700s. In 1822, the Moravian Elders decided that the citizens of Salem were "getting too familiar" with the slaves of their community. One of the steps taken to remedy this problem was to build the slaves their own church. In 1823, the logs of the first "Negro" or "African" church were laid. This church was intended to be used by the African community living in and around Salem. Slaves and freemen alike worshiped in this humble church for about the next 40 years. Eventually, a larger church was needed, and in 1861, on an adjacent site, a new brick church was built. It was named St. Philip's Moravian, and is to this date the oldest standing African-American church structure in North Carolina. In 1890, an addition was added that covered a part of the old "stranger's graveyard." In 1952, the congregation chose to build another church in the Happy Hill community, and in the late 1960s it moved once more. St. Philip's Moravian is still an active congregation. In the upcoming years, Old Salem plans to reconstruct the log church and restore the brick church. This major project is essential in interpreting the lives and experiences of the African Americans in the community of Salem during the 19th century. (COS.)

Two
WINSTON AND SALEM:
HOME FIRES BURNING

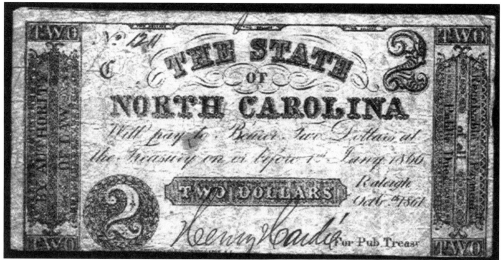

THE RICH, AS WELL AS THE POOR, were tremendously affected by the economic destruction of
the Civil War. Food was scarce, and money was inflated (a silver dollar placed in the offering
plate at Home Church was estimated to be worth $40). The Moravian Church lost the funds
that had been built up by the sale of Wachovia lands. Salt sold for $20 per sack and corn was
$10 per bushel. Soldiers wrote letters home seeking news of crops and cattle. Heavy losses in
the price of tobacco ruined many families. Women took to the fields and the bartering system
became a major enterprise. In 1863, a mob of women arrived in Salisbury armed with hatchets,
demanding flour that the shopkeepers were hoarding for higher profits. When the women were
not taken seriously with their demands, they proceeded to break into the mercantile shops with
their weapons, holding the shopkeepers at arms length until the badly needed flour, molasses,
and salt were procured.

1] EMMA CHRISTINE FRIES BAHNSON   2] LAURA CAROLINE VOGLER

3] JOSEPH ANTHONY AND LOUISA WILSON BITING

1] EMMA CHRISTINE FRIES BAHNSON

Emma Christine Fries Bahnson was the second wife of Dr. Henry Bahnson. During one of the Confederate veteran reunions, Dr. Henry Bahnson publicly honored and recognized the sacrifices of the women during the Civil War. The following excerpt is from his Address to the Confederate Veterans:

". . . But we can speak in unstilted praise of the best and greatest glory of the South— the women of the war. Their soft voices inspired us, their prayers followed us and shielded us from temptation and harm. We witnessed their spartan courage and self-sacrifice in every stage of the war. We saw them send their husbands and their fathers, their brothers and their sons and their sweethearts, to the front, tempering their joys in the hour of triumph, cheering and comforting them in the days of despair and disaster. Freely they gave of their abundance, and gladly endured privation and direst poverty that the men in the field might be clothed and fed. Their days of unaccustomed toil were saddened with anxious suspense, and the lonely, prayerful vigils of the night afforded no rest. They nursed the sick and wounded; they soothed the dying; and in the last stages of the war, when all was lost but honor, we were made to marvel at their saintly spirit of martyrdom, standing as it were almost neck deep in the desolation around them, bravely facing their fate, while the light of heaven illuminated their divinely beautiful countenances."

2] LAURA CAROLINE VOGLER

Laura Caroline Vogler (October 23, 1829–November 3, 1894) was the eldest daughter of Nathanael and Anna (Fischel) Vogler. After completing her studies at Salem Academy, she married John William Beck on December 30, 1863. At the Blantyre Wayside Hospital, which was located near her home, Laura cooked for injured men and nursed them back to health. Wayside hospitals were essential for the soldiers, who were constantly on the road and often not very close to military or private hospitals. Other women from Salem who served as volunteer nurses were Mrs. Eliza Kremer, Miss Lizetta Stewart, Miss L. Shaub, and Miss Margaret Clewell. The following letter from Laura to her sister Maria describes some of her ordeals:

"Fauquier Co., VA Oct. 6, 1861 Dear Sister, I received your letter last evening and was glad to hear that you were all well and now I must tell you what we are doing. We are in a large stone house have to cook for about forty men well and sick, well men come to nurse the sick, we go and feed them three times a day, talk to them and try to make them believe they are getting better, in fact we have none that are very sick. Four men died this morning but they were so far gone when they brought them that we could do nothing for them, they were Craver from Davidson and Rasch from Rockingham. Julius came to camp on last Tuesday, he looked pale but says he is most well. We have plenty to cook, first rare beef and muffins, we also have all day to do cooking. I have baked light bread three times, but men would rather eat corn bread. We have very nice corn meal and if we ask them that can come to the table, what they want, they say mush and milk for breakfast, dinner and supper. Some eat slop if we tell them its good. They say fried rice and I don't wonder cooking it in them old rusty camp kettles. I am glad that I came along with the others if I do have to work

hard, for when the men come to the table, that are nothing but skin and bones and eat like if it tasted so good to them, it does my heart good to see them eat. R Chitty is with us, not sick but to wait on the sick and help us. Tell his sister that he looks very well and his cough is most gone. I told him if he wanted anything to let us know, he is not shy at all, in fact well sound like if had known one another all our lives. Connie Willie is very well, says he has been sick a day since he left home. It is most time to get supper and we have old bread so we thought we would pour riders for supper and mush and milk. Dr. Schaffner is the head man of the house, and does all he can for us. Oct. 7. Three o'clock in the afternoon, just done washing our dinner dishes. Col. Kirkland ate dinner with us. Mrs. Smith sent a negro woman to wash our clothes. Maggie and Litte have gone to the stove, cooking pays well to see how much most of our men improve, seven more came yesterday evening, but very bad. It has been very warm for the last few days, but is cooler today. The woods are quite green yet. I wish you could see the cattle and sheep. This morning we heard the cannon firing, but have not heard where it was. Sandy Gieger is here but is not very sick, but complains a good deal. Every evening before we go to bed we have to kill spiders, you never saw the like in all your live, they are as large as my thumb. Oct. 9 Baking bread record time today have not time to write any more, am well. Write soon, Laura." (HEV and PCVM.)

3] JOSEPH ANTHONY AND LOUISA WILSON BITTING

Joseph Anthony Bitting (February 7, 1820–January 6, 1901) was born in Stokes County, and was a descendant of some of the first settlers of the area. During the war, he tried to look after the comfort and needs of the families of the soldiers. As a merchant, he was able to provide supplies to the families in his community during the hardships of the war. All his efforts were quashed when Stoneman's raiders pillaged Joseph's home and store as they tore through Germanton. Joseph's wife, Louisa Wilson Bitting, was born at Bethania in Stokes County to Dr. George Follet Wilson and Henrietta Hauser. In 1898, Louisa helped organize the James B. Gordon Chapter of the United Daughters of the Confederacy, located in Forsyth County. On May 6, 1898, she was accepted as one of the charter members of this organization. She joined on the military service of her brother, Maj. Reuben Wilson of the 1st Battalion, NC Sharpshooters. Mrs. Bitting was prominent in the Winston community through her social, religious, and philanthropic affairs. Joseph died in Forsyth County and is buried in the Bitting family plot at the Salem Cemetery. (JSC.)

4] MRS. ELIZA W. KREEMER

Mrs. Eliza W. Kreemer taught school in the first public schoolhouse in Winston during the Civil War. As early as the 1840s, public education was not taken as seriously as some believed it should. Mr. Calvin H. Wiley, who served as the first state superintendent of common schools from 1853 to 1865, revolutionized the North Carolina Common School system. Enrollment grew, and the number of "certified teachers" increased from 800 to 2,286. (NCR.)

4] Mrs. Eliza W. Kreemer

5] Maria Elizabeth Vogler

6] Sara Elvina Kreeger Eaton

5] Maria Elizabeth Vogler

Maria Elizabeth Vogler (March 5, 1830–October 31, 1910) was born to Nathanael and Anna Maria (Fishel) Vogler. After attending the Salem School for Girls, she chose teaching at the Female Academy as her vocation. In 1882, after almost 30 years of teaching, she retired to her mother's home. Maria was ever diligent in her correspondence to her beloved brother Julius and many other Vogler relatives as well. Fiercely dedicated to her family, she lived at home and nursed both her elderly mother and her brother Julius. She was the first in her family to start documenting the Vogler family history back to the old country. What she collected in her research enabled Vogler researchers to continue to build a remarkable database of families from all over the world. She is buried in the Salem Cemetery. (HEV and PCVM.)

6] Sara Elvina Kreeger Eaton

Sara Elvina Kreeger Eaton was born on May 2, 1821, to Jacob and Mary "Polly" Fulp Kreeger (it was Jacob who deeded the land for the Mt. Pleasant Methodist Church in Tobaccoville). On October 24, 1846, Sara married John Henry Eaton. The 1860 Forsyth County census lists Sara and John as having two daughters, Mary Frances and Temperance Mahaly. When John enlisted for the war, Sara became solely responsible for the care of their children, as well as their farm. In December 1863, John joined the 9th Regiment, Co. G (formerly the 1st Regiment, NC Cavalry), and in October 1864 he transferred to Co. B of the 21st Regiment, NC Troops. His descendants believe he lost his horse during a battle, which would explain the change in his military records from cavalry to infantry. He came home from the war one weekend, and when Sara and the children woke up, they found him sitting under a tree in the yard. He wouldn't come into the house and left early the next day to return to his regiment. He died of "disease" in Petersburg on April 1, 1865—the day before the Yankees broke through the Confederate lines. Sara and her daughters fended for themselves during the war. The stories of their hardships were handed down through the generations. One particular story tells of how they had to take their horses and cows deep into the woods to hide them from Yankee soldiers. They also buried some of their "valuables" to keep them from the marauding soldiers. The Eatons lived between Crooked Run Creek and the Mt. Pleasant Methodist Church in Tobaccoville. Sara is buried there, but John is believed to be buried in a mass grave near Petersburg. (SBR.)

7] Sheriff Mathias and Catherine Masten

Sheriff Mathias Masten (December 3, 1821–February 27, 1873) was born to Darius and Mary Fair Masten. On February 10, 1848, he married Catherine Masten, his second cousin, the daughter of William and Lucy Richards Masten. Mathias was no doubt one of the most prominent and widely known men in the Forsyth County area. He was an ardent Republican, and was never defeated in his campaigns for the position of sheriff of Forsyth County. When he died, he was serving his 12th year in that public office. During the Civil War, he was tireless in his responsibilities as sheriff to protect and uphold the law in Forsyth County. His home was always open to Confederate officers, but he made no apologies for being a Union supporter,

7] SHERIFF MATHIAS AND CATHERINE MASTEN

even under the threat of imprisonment in Castle Thunder. As kind as he was to all, he was not one to be toyed with. One day when Yankee raiders came through Kernersville, they kidnapped his son, John Henry Masten. When word finally reached him, he immediately rode hard and many miles until he caught up with the bushwackers who held his son. His terms were simple. They were to release his son or "regardless of what happened to him, some of them were certainly going to end their earthly life then and there." He returned home with John Henry unharmed. On February 27, 1873, Mathias Masten passed away at his residence near Salem. The *Union Republican* reported his death as follows:

> "When permitted no longer to muster his Regiment under the Stars and Stripes he took the Old Flag to his home where it was cherished and revered as a relic of the Revolution. It was the shrine at which many a patriotic tear was shed. During the four years of horrid war to destroy the Union, his home was the resort of Patriotic Unionists who revered the Flag of their country. He was one of a committee of five Southern Unionist, who at the risk of being sent to Castle Thunder, or some other Castle, opened a correspondence with the leading men and thereby induce the Governor with the Legislature to call a sentiment by petition to relieve North Carolina from the dire ruin secession had precipitated on the country. In the death of Mathias Masten, Forsyth County mourns the loss of one of her most gifted sons. Self made and without the advantages of a liberal education, but possessing great acuteness of intellect and popularity of manner and a large fund of information, he was an able debater, popular speaker and formidable politician as many a political opponent learned to his sorrow on the hustings. On Friday the 28th his remains were followed to their last resting place in Middlefork Burial Grounds amid an immence concourse of sympathetic friends and acquaintances." (SSD.)

8] AUGUSTUS VOGLE

Augustus Fogle was born in 1820 in Salem. He served 20 years as steward of the Salem Female Academy, and was exempted from military service during the Civil War "in order that he might continue to serve the daughters of the South." Augustus, who was responsible for providing food and supplies for the resident students, travelled around the countryside searching for food. He slept in a room provided for him near the Main Hall, where he could keep watch over the welfare and property of both the school and the ladies. On April 2, 1865, news of the impending arrival of Union soldiers sent the Winston and Salem communities into a tailspin. John Blackburn, clerk of court, distributed court papers and books to various homes. Cotton, cloth, and horses were hidden. Salem's principal hid money and jewelry of the students in the cellar of his home. Two horses were hid under the Main Hall. Colonel Palmer and the 10th Ohio Volunteer Cavalry arrived on May 14, 1865, and took charge of the two townships. Thousands of Union soldiers made camp about where the Reynolds Tobacco Company's plants once were, and extended up to where the "dry bridge crosses the railroad tracks at Liberty Street," which at the time was mostly woods. In order to subdue any cause for alarm within the two townships, sentry guards were placed around them. Augustus noticed that the young soldier who had been detailed to guard Salem Academy's Main Hall was so exhausted that he was scarcely able to walk. After much insistence and kindness, the young guard accepted an invitation to rest in Augustus's bed "just a few minutes." As the young boy slept, Augustus took his gun and maintained the watch in his place. He later served as the fourth sheriff of Forsyth County for six years, as well as mayor of Salem. His sons, Charles A. and Christian H. Fogle, founded the Fogle Brothers Company, which was instrumental in erecting many of the first buildings during Winston's infancy as a new township. (NCR.)

9] FRANCIS LEVIN FRIES

Francis Levin Fries (October 10, 1812–August 1, 1863) was born in Salem. On May 24, 1838, he married Lisetta Maria Vogler (March 3, 1820–October 23, 1903), the daughter of John and Christina Spach Vogler. Francis was a prominent citizen of Salem. He served his community as a pioneer manufacturer and a respected civic leader. Years before the Civil War, he traveled north to learn more about the mills located there. He immediately recognized the types of machinery and business methods needed to run a successful mill in Salem. He ingeniously invented new machinery to make the mill run more effectively, and then organized the Salem Cotton Manufacturing Company. His most successful venture was the ability to mechanically card the wool needed for weaving and spinning. In 1846, his brother Henry became his partner, and the two built the famous firm of F. and H. Fries. At the outbreak of the Civil War, the Fries factory wove and supplied massive amounts of wool and cotton to the Confederate Army. In 1861, Henry corresponded to North Carolina Governor Henry T. Clark concerning his problems adequately supplying the army:

> "Salem N.C. Nov 18, 1861 Gov. Henry T. Clark Raleigh, NC Dear Sir, I dislike exceedingly to intrude so often on your valuable time, but as I have never done so on my own account, & the State is interested as well as ourselves in the subject now on my mind. I know you will pardon me for this letter. All who know the circumstances will bear us witness, that to the neglect of our old customers & of our interest we have

8] AUGUSTUS FOGLE

9] FRANCIS LEVIN FRIES

10] A CONFEDERATE REUNION

from the beginning of our troubles, made all our business yield to the demands of the army. This applies to the cotton & wool mills of F. & H. Fries as well as to the touyars [?] of Fries & Co. which belongs to me. Everyone has tried to stand aside, where the State, The Confederacy or parties making wool for the army applied for any thing we had. Now our only hope for wool articles is a supply from Texas, & brother has for two months been out trying to get up stock to enable us to keep our promises for army supplies. With much labor & great expense he has partially succeeded, but it appears impossible to get what has been thus secured. Nothing is coming through, & to say I see that the Memphis & Charleston RR refuses to carry for anyone except government, which explains why we get no materials. The army must of course have provisions munitions of war, but I doubt whether with out shoes or clothing it will long be efficient. I leave it to your wisdom whether any or what steps should be taken to the State authorities to remedy the evil. This is certain—if the government forbids the transportation of raw materials the woolen mills & many of the sole [?] brothers [?] tourgard [?] in the Atlantic States will soon be compelled to suspend operations. The loss of the manufacturers, or the suffering of hands thrown out of employment should weigh nothing if conflicting with the public good, but what will the army do if the making of clothing ceases? Might I intimate that a coup d'etat from you to the authorities of Tennessee & Lo Co. [?] & of the Confederate States, setting for the above views & such others as your good judgment will rendiy [readily?] suggest, would not fail to show them the importance if expediting the transportatior of raw materials used for shoes, [harnesses?], clothing, etc. & an order from such authorities to the Roads under their contract would keep all mills running. Yours truly, H. Fries."

Henry and his wife are buried in the Salem Cemetery in Winston-Salem. (NCR.)

10] A Confederate Reunion

A Confederate reunion was held in Winston-Salem on September 24, 1930. From left to right are S.B. Carlisle, W.S. Grissom, Capt. N.W. Bernhardt, J.A. McAskill, M.D. McNeill, Mrs. W.A. Smith, T.N. Alexander, W.G. Johnson, John Henry Shore, and W.M. Barwick. Maj. Gen. W.A. Smith is seated. (NCR.)

11] The Forsyth Riflemen

The Forsyth Riflemen were organized on February 15, 1812, in Germantown. The Riflemen were the first permanent military organization in the county. After serving in the War of 1812, they served in the Mexican War, and were attached with the 1st Battalion, NC Volunteers, and the 21st Regiment, NC Troops, during the Civil War, as well as the 30th Infantry in World War I. During times of turbulence in the county, they often acted as reinforcements for the police. (NCR.)

11] THE FORSYTH RIFLEMEN

12] AUGUSTUS FOGLE

13] ELIAS ALEXANDER VOGLER

12] SAMUEL HOLMES SMITH

Samuel Holmes Smith was born in Wadesboro on September 15, 1846. He attended school at the Oak Ridge Institute in Kernersville, Forsyth County. Before he had finished his education, however, he left school to go into business with his brother-in-law, J.W. Lambeth, manufacturing bayonets, scabbards, and cartridge boxes for the Confederate government. Samuel eventually enlisted with the 1st NC Artillery (10th NC Troops), also known as Southerland's Battery, NC Light Artillery. In 1875, he moved to Winston, Forsyth County. He served several years on the board of aldermen, and two terms as mayor of the city. Before his last term as mayor expired, President Cleveland appointed him as postmaster. In 1883, he reorganized the Forsyth Riflemen, and was elected captain of the company. He served in this position until being promoted to major of the 3rd Regiment of the State Guard. Colonel Smith was one of the prime movers in organizing Norfleet Camp No. 436, UCV, and was elected their first adjutant. (CVM.)

13] ELIAS ALEXANDER VOGLER

Elias Alexander Vogler (October 31, 1825–November 17, 1876), the son of John and Christina Vogler, was a very talented and highly respected citizen of Salem. He specialized in miniature portraits, but his primary wealth was gained from merchandising. Elias wholesaled and retailed products ranging from dried fruits to tombstones, from farm produce and machinery to railroad stock. He was also very community minded, serving as a justice of the peace and as mayor of Salem. Although he did not serve in the war, he certainly was a huge asset to the continual needs of the hometown soldiers. Many times throughout the conflict, he coordinated the collection of clothing, shoes, and food for the soldiers of the 21st Regiment. As president of the board of sustenance, he coordinated his 17 sub-agents throughout the county to see that every soldier's family was provided for, as well as some 1,200 other persons in need of food. He tirelessly laid in provisions, anticipating shortages, and always distributed the supplies in an honest and fair manner. Through his talent for planning and business, his devotion of time and means, and his liberality, he secured the cooperation and respect of the entire community. The November 8, 1861 issue of the *People's Press* reflects the many advertisements Vogler printed during the course of the war:

> "*Wanted—Large Quantity of Good Country Jeans or Linsey to clothe men who have sacrificed home and its comforts for camp life. The highest market price will be paid in cash for all such goods by bringing them to E.A. Vogler store in the next few weeks. The color is immaterial. Country merchants are respectfully requested to retain and get as much of the above named goods as possible.*"

Elias died on November 17, 1876, in Salem. (FGM and PCVM.)

14] THE JAS. B. GORDON CHAPTER OF THE UDC

In 1898, Dr. James A. Blum, a Confederate veteran from Salem, requested that a number of ladies meet to discuss organizing a chapter of the United Daughters of the Confederacy.

14] THE JAS. B GORDON CHAPTER
OF THE UDC

15] RUEBEN E. WILSON

Mrs. Joseph A. Bitting suggested that the chapter be named after Brig.-Gen. James B. Gordon of Wilkes County. On March 30, 1898, a charter for the Forsyth County UDC chapter was approved by the National UDC office. The first project the ladies chose was that of erecting a monument honoring the Confederate soldiers. Dr. Blum presented the design, and the members started their fund-raising campaign. To raise part of $3,000 needed, the James B. Gordon Chapter featured the first moving picture ever shown in Winston-Salem at the old armory, which was located where the R.J. Reynolds Headquarters building now stands. Through hard work and community donation, the money was raised. Two years later, on October 3, 1905, the erection of the monument took place on the northwest corner of the courthouse square, facing due north, from whence the enemy came. In honor of the unveiling, W.T. Vogler & Sons, who were jewelers in Salem, "fitted up an attractive Confederate Window" in which were displayed relics of the Civil War; i.e. an old rifle used by Mr. Vogler, Confederate flags, and Confederate money of various denominations. Placed in the center of the display was suspended the "battle and time scarred coats and blanket that were used by Dr. J.A. Blum."

15] RUEBEN E. WILSON

Reuben E. Wilson (December 31, 1840–March 8, 1907) was born in Stokes County. He volunteered with the Yadkin Gray Eagles (Co. B, 21st NC Infantry), which was organized on May 12, 1861. By April of 1862, he was elected to serve as first lieutenant, and by June of that same year, he was promoted to captain. On April 26–28, 1862, Co. B was transferred to the newly organized 1st Battalion, N.C. Sharpshooters. The Sharpshooters were made up of two companies (Co. B and Co. E, which ultimately became Co. A and B respectively) of the 21st Regiment. This was a small battalion, but one critical to the regiment. During most of 1864, Reuben commanded the battalion in the capacity of senior captain. During the fall of 1864 and early 1865, the Sharpshooters scouted the woods of North Carolina and Virginia in order to flush out and apprehend deserters. On April 2, 1865, during the Battle of Petersburg, he was hit with a mini-ball that broke both bones of his right arm. The shattering grapeshot cut off his leg below the knee. He was hospitalized at Manchester, Virginia, until April 29, 1865. Ten days later, he was arrested by Federal military authorities, and was incarcerated at Libby Prison in Richmond. His official charge was that of intercepting and shooting deserters. Reuben remained in the Raleigh penitentiary until December 20, 1865. After a trial and acquittal, he was allowed to return home. In 1910, the *Confederate Veteran* magazine reported his death as follows:

> "*Maj. R.E. Wilson, of Winston, N.C. [it should be noted that no official sources indicate Wilson ever received a major's commission], who was as faithful a Confederate as ever wore the gray, died a long while ago; but nobody gave notice to the VETERAN, although he was so faithful a friend and patron. At Reunions as long as able to go he made his headquarters at the same place with the VETERAN, and watched with deepest solicitude everything that concerned it.*"

He died March 8, 1907, in Forsyth, North Carolina. (CUM.)

Three

CALL OUT THE MILITIA:
PROTECTING THE HOME FRONT

MADISON CALVIN DEAN was born near Kernersville on October 25, 1832. In 1857, he married Faitha Imes in Davidson County. To this marriage were born six daughters and two sons. At age 32, Madison was called to service. He enlisted in Wake County on March 18, 1864, with Co. F, 6th NC State Troops. He experienced battle at Plymouth, Cold Harbor, Kernstown, Hatcher's Run, and Sayler's Creek, and was paroled at Greensboro on May 29, 1865. After the war, he returned to farming. It is said he plowed a 10-acre field shortly before his 96th birthday. He is buried at Piney Grove United Methodist Church in Kernersville. Shown here, from left to right, are the following: (sitting) Madison Calvin Dean, Faitha Imes Dean, David Dean, and Mary Dean Motsinger; (standing) Annie Dean Waggoner, Josie Dean Hepler, Ellen Dean, Joseph Dean, Lula Dean Smith, and Victoria Dean. (PSB.)

1] LOUIS MARTIN VEST

2] THOMAS LENOIR GWYN

3] ROBERT CHURCH

4] SAMUEL ALSPAUGH

1] LOUIS MARTIN VEST

Lewis Martin Vest was born on November 28, 1834, to William Vest and Nancy Ogburn. Lewis and his two brothers, James W. and Wesley, operated the stagecoach route from Tobaccoville to Bristol. This service exempted them from military duty during the Civil War. On November 27, 1862, Lewis married Mary Jane Schaub, who was born on February 22, 1840, to William Samuel Schaub and Anna Eliza Hauser. She was the sister of Capt. Winborn Benjamin Schaub. (AMVR.)

2] THOMAS LENOIR GWYN

Thomas Lenoir Gwyn was born on November 9, 1842, in Elkin to Richard and Elizabeth Martin Hunt Gwyn. Richard owned his own mercantile business in Jonesville. Both the Gwyn and Hunt families were large landowners. Prior to the war, Thomas was a student in the Jonesville Academy. It was during this time he enlisted with Co. A, NC 2nd Infantry Battalion, commanded by Capt. G.C. Stowe and Maj. J.C. McRay. Thomas ambitiously assisted in raising this company, and was duly elected as lieutenant. With his regiment, he traveled to Camp Vance in Burke County to drill. He first experienced action in the siege of Knoxville. During the Battle of Cansbys Creek, his regiment found themselves surrounded by the enemy. In the absence of the captain and the first lieutenant, Thomas led his company in a dash through the enemy's line. He escaped his enemies, but not without his ear becoming damaged from a bullet. With eight of his companions, he returned to Salisbury, where he was commissioned adjutant of the Sr. Reserves and was detailed to guard the prison. He remained in this position until the close of the war. On April 3, 1867, he married Amelia J. Dickenson of Hardeman County, Tennessee, the daughter of James and Julia (Thurman) Dickenson. In 1877, Thomas, his cousin Richard, and their cousin Alexander Chatham started a woolen mill at Elkin, known now as the Chatham Manufacturing Company. (NCR.)

3] ROBERT CHURCH

Robert Church moved his family from Stokes County to Morehead City prior to the beginning of the war. Leaving his wife and five children, he enlisted in Carteret County on July 5, 1861, joining Co. F, Andrew's Battery, 10th Regiment, NC State Troops (1st Regiment, NC Artillery). Prior to his enlistment, he made his living as a baker. Unfortunately for him, his baking talents were a total fiasco with his fellow soldiers. According to Troy Church, Robert's great-grandson, the fort Robert was stationed at was over-stocked with flour, resulting in a disproportionate amount of the required daily ration being given to the soldiers. When Colonel White learned that Robert was a baker by trade, he ordered that an oven be built and that Robert be responsible for baking loaves. Initially, the soldiers thought this was a grand idea, as they would no longer have to do their own baking. Unfortunately, Robert's skill as a civilian baker did not measure up to what was required in a military environment. The loaves were so hard and inedible that it was suggested they be used for ammunition. Against all pleas from his field and staff officers, Colonel White refused to withdraw Robert from baking duty. Realizing that the troops were close to a "baking rebellion," the officers sided with their men and demanded that the flour appropriations be reinstated or they would seize the flour.

Colonel White in turn threatened the officers with arrest, but could find no one to carry out his orders. In the end Colonel White granted his men their flour rations and Robert's military baking career ended. It is believed that he was killed during the Battle of Fort Fisher. (TC.)

4] SAMUEL ALSPAUGH

Samuel Alspaugh, the son of Rev. John and Elizabeth Lashmit Alspaugh, served in the NC Militia of Forsyth County, 71st Regiment, 17th Brigade. On April 12, 1862, he was promoted from captain to lieutenant colonel when Mathias Masten was "thrown out by Division." (LA.)

5] WILEY A. AND FRANCES REBECCA YOUNTS NIFONG

Wiley A. Nifong (March 13, 1845–October 4, 1912) was born in Davidson County to Robert Nifong and Sarah Weir Nifong. On March 18, 1865, he enlisted in Co. C., 49th Regiment NC Infantry. On April 3, 1865, he sustained a gunshot wound to the left shoulder, and was furloughed for 30 days. On December 21, 1871, Wiley married Frances Rebecca Younts, the daughter of Samuel and Anna Grimes Younts. He died on October 4, 1912, and his wife died on August 30, 1910. Both are buried in the Oakwood Cemetery in High Point. (BL.)

6] WILLIAM YOUNG

William Young (May 28, 1815–April 3, 1882) was born in Stokes County to Benjamin and Judith Duncan Young. On May 26, 1846, he married Elizabeth "Betsy" Wood, the daughter of John and Nancy Tilley Wood. To their union were born seven children. By 1864, the Confederate Army was experiencing heavy losses and began conscripting both young and old for reinforcements. On February 17, 1864, the Confederate Congress passed a new enrollment act requiring men between the ages of 45 and 50 to enlist in the Senior Reserves. Under the appointment of Col. Charles E. Shober, Lt. Col. J.A. Barrett, and Maj. J.C. Dobbins, the 7th Regiment, Sr. Reserves organized that following July; it came to be known after the war as the 77th Regiment. William was assigned to Capt. William H. Watt's Company on June 23, 1864, in Germantown. This unit traveled to Georgia and Florida from January to March 1865. They returned during the Carolina's Campaign under Gen. Joseph Johnston's Army of Tennessee, where they participated in the Battles of Averasboro and Bentonville, North Carolina. William died on April 3, 1882, in Stokes County. (SC.)

7] ISAAC PETREE

Isaac Petree (February 25, 1819–October 9, 1893) was born in Stokes County and died in Forsyth County. On March 12, 1845, he married Sophia Shamel in Stokes County. He and

5] WILEY A. AND FRANCES REBECCA YOUNTS NIFONG

6] WILLIAM YOUNG

7] ISAAC PETREE

his wife had the following known children: James A., Ellen, Isaac Nathaniel, Jeremiah, and Elmira. Isaac was a member of Co. G, 7th NC Sr. Reserves. He reported to Captain Eli E. Holland on June 23, 1864. The muster rolls described Isaac as being 5'11" tall, with fair complexion, light blonde hair, and blue eyes. He was a farmer by occupation, and was 45 years old when he enlisted as a private. (NRP.)

8] CAPT. ROBERT F. DALTON AND MEMBERS OF HIS FAMILY

Capt. Robert F. Dalton poses with his family in Danbury in 1870. From left to right are as follows: (front row) 66-year-old Absolom Bostic Dalton (Robert's father), John Fox Dalton, and David Nicholas Dalton; (back row) Gabriel Dalton, George Dalton, and Capt. Robert F. Dalton. On May 30, 1864, 400 men, both young and old, joined together at Camp Holmes near Raleigh to create Co. C, 4th Battalion, NC Jr. Reserves, under the command of Capt. Robert F. Dalton, Frst. Lt. G. Mason, and Sec. Lts. G.W. Yancy and J.H. Shackleford. Upon reaching Camp Holmes, Captain Dalton's company joined with Co. A from Guilford County, Co. B from Alamance and Forsyth Counties, and Co. D from Rockingham County. After its organization, the 4th Battalion joined with the 7th and 8th Battalions to create the 3rd Regiment of Jr. Reserves. (SSD.)

9] JOHN LUNSFORD AND MARTHA LOUISE BURCHETTE BUTNER

John Lunsford Butner (February 19, 1847–June 10, 1925) was born in the home his father built beside Crooked Run Creek (present-day Butner Road in Tobaccoville, North Carolina). He was the 10th of 12 children born to Jacob and Elizabeth Hauser Butner. Four months after his 17th birthday, John went to Camp Holmes near Raleigh, enlisting with Co. B., 4th Infantry Battalion, NC Jr. Reserves, for the duration of the war. The 4th Battalion was led by Maj. John M. Reece of Greensboro. John Butner served guard and picket duty in the eastern part of North Carolina—primarily at Sugar Loaf on the Cape Fear River near Fort Fisher. He participated in several skirmishes, including one in Belfield, Virginia, in December 1864, preventing the Federal forces from cutting the railroad link between Weldon, North Carolina, and Petersburg, Virginia. On Christmas Day, 1864, during the attack on Fort Fisher, he was captured and transported to Point Lookout. He remained there until his release on June 23, 1865, after signing the Oath of Allegiance. John married Martha Louise Burchette of East Bend, North Carolina. The couple had 12 children, and is buried at Mt. Pleasant Methodist Church in Tobaccoville. (SBR.)

10] MEMBERS OF THE 72ND NC REGIMENT

Members of the 72nd NC Regiment pose for a photographer. They are, from left to right, as follows: (bottom row) Sec. Lt. David Settle Reid, Orderly Sgt. C.W. Taylor, and Pvt. J.L. McGimpsey; (middle row) Sec. Lt. H.W. Connelly, Col. John W. Hinsdale, and Sec. Lt. J.M. Bandy; (top row) Frst. Lt. W.W. King, Lt. Col. W. Foster French, and Sec. Lt. Jno. W. Harper. (NCR.)

8] Capt. Robert F Dalton and Members of His Family

9] John Lunsford and Martha Louise Burchette Butner

10] MEMBERS OF THE 72ND NC REGIMENT

11] JOSEPH HENRY COVINGTON

12] DAVID SETTLE REID

11] JOSEPH HENRY COVINGTON

Joseph Henry Covington (October 9, 1845–September 7, 1899), the son of Josiah and Caroline Brown Covington, was born in Stokes County. On May 27, 1864, at the age of 18, he enlisted for service at Camp Holmes, Raleigh, and joined the 4th Battalion, Jr. Reserves. This battalion of 400 young men, consolidated with the 7th and 8th Battalions, formed the 3rd Regiment, Jr. Reserves, also known as the 72nd Regiment. The commander was Capt. Robert F. Dalton of Stokes County. Joseph was assigned to Co. C, which was organized at Camp Holmes three days after he enlisted, and included men from both Stokes and Person Counties. The Jr. Reserves fought bravely during the attack on Fort Fisher in December of 1864. They also served in the Carolina's Campaign (February-April 1865), which included the Battle of Bentonville (March 19–21, 1865). Covington survived the war, but his two older brothers were not so fortunate: Peter J., of the Co. F., 21st Regiment, died near Manassas in 1861, and Thomas, of the Co. H., 53rd Regiment, died at Richmond in 1865. On February 13, 1883, Joseph married Gillie Susan Williams, the daughter of Charles M. and Julia Fulp Williams of Stokes County. He died on September 7, 1899, in Stokes County. (SC.)

12] DAVID SETTLE REID

David Settle Reid (April 28, 1847–December 31, 1943) was born in Guilford County to Anselm and Martha Peoples Reid. At the age of 17, he joined Co. A, 4th Battalion, NC Infantry, and by the close of the war he had reached the rank of lieutenant colonel. On January 25, 1911, David married his second wife, Miss Allie Gooch. He ran a successful china and mercantile business in Winston-Salem. This photograph was taken at the Confederate Memorial Service held in the Salem Cemetery on May 8, 1939. When David died on December 31, 1943, he was the last Confederate veteran in Forsyth County. (NCR.)

13] TENNYSON JARVIS

Tennyson Jarvis (1827–March 25, 1863) was born in Forsyth County to James and Sarah Cheshire Jarvis. Tennyson and his wife, Mary Jane Boyer, had eight children. On July 4, 1862, he enlisted with the 57th NC Infantry, organized by Capt. James E. Mann, the pastor of Winston's Methodist Episcopal Church. By September 22, 1862, Tennyson was listed on the sick list report. Apparently, the rough conditions of the training camp had been bad for his health. The 57th Regiment was ordered north to Richmond in September of 1862 to provide additional reinforcements. Tennyson, still sick at this time, traveled to Richmond. He was again hospitalized from September 1862 until February 1863. During this time, he was sent home with four weeks sick leave. He walked all the way home through the bitter cold, fording the James River as well as other small streams. When he arrived home he was near death. Overstaying his sick leave, a troop of mounted horsemen was sent to return him to his regiment in Richmond. Tennyson was still very ill. His last words to his wife were "You'll never see me alive again." He died in Chimborazo Hospital in Richmond on March 25, 1863. The records state that the cause of death was measles. His body was shipped home by rail to Greensboro. The following is one of the letters Mary Boyer Jarvis wrote to her husband:

"Dear husband I take my pen in hand to let you know that myself and children are all well hopeing these few lines may find you improveing I have not received any letter from you since you was in Richmond I suppose you have been too sick to write to me. Augustus Vogler has let me know how you are he sent me word in a letter he wrote to his father dated Mar. the 24th which gave me great satisfaction to hear that you was some better, I hope you will be well enough to write to me soon as I am verry desirous to hear from you & to know how you are. I have tried to get William to go with me to see you or go himself but I could not get him to go no way so no more at present but remain your affectionate wife until Death . . . Mary Jarvis." (FJM.)

14] ALEXANDER CHRISTOPHER "SANDY" VOGLER

Alexander Christopher "Sandy" Vogler was born on March 13, 1832, one of nine children born to Nathanael and Anna Maria Fischel Vogler. In his youth he learned the trade of cabinetmaking from John D. Siewers of Salem. He then traveled to Macon, Georgia, to master his skills. On October 26, 1859, he married Antoinette Susanna Shultz Hauser. During the Civil War, Alexander was assigned to the Home Guard, 64th Battalion, under the command of Colonel J. Masten of Winston, Forsyth County. This battalion was initially responsible for the safety of Forsyth County, but many of the soldiers were re-assigned to defend other towns and regions as a result of the heavy casualties in the Battle of Gettysburg. In 1867, Alexander opened his first furniture store in Salem. In addition to all of the beautifully hand-crafted bureaus, chairs, tables, etc., one could also make a selection from his exclusive line of hand-tooled coffins. In the early 1870s, Vogler included the art of undertaking in his business. This was the beginning of the Vogler Funeral Home, which is still in existence today. Alexander and his wife had three children: William Edward, Mary Anna, and Francis (Frank) Henry Vogler. The following letter was written by Vogler to his sister on December 1, 1864:

"Camp Near Kinston, Dear Sister, I received your letter day before yesterday evening & was very glad to hear from you all. I had been very uneasy about Mother. I hope Mother & Father are both well by this time.... You asked me if being company commissary did not excuse me from guard duty. It excuses me from 2 hours drill every day & from picket duty. I must drill 2 hours every day, attend dress parade every evening to stand guard duty every 3 days, 8 hours out of 24, it keeps me busy pretty much all the time, we have to carry our fire wood about 1/2 mile, pine is the best wood we can get we are all getting smoked pretty black.... Christ Pfohl will start home in the morning. I will send this by him, he has a sick furlough, there have been 145 furlough to discharged from this regiment. It is very doubtful whether we get home by Christmas. Please write soon again. Give all my love to all. Your Brother, Sandy." (HEV and PCVM.)

15] JOHN BENNETT AND MARY FRANCES EATON SPRINKLE

John Bennett Sprinkle (October 22, 1846–February 13, 1933) and his wife, Mary Frances Eaton Sprinkle, are shown here at the United Confederate Veteran Reunion in Alabama in 1931. John Bennet Sprinkle was the third child of John (Jack) and Martha (Patty) Newsom Sprinkle of the Dozier area of Forsyth County. On May 24, 1864, John traveled to Camp

13] TENNYSON JARVIS

14] ALEXANDER CHRISTOPHER
"SANDY" VOGLER

15] JOHN BENNETT AND
MARY FRANCES EATON SPRINKLE

16] PLEASANT HENDERSON HANES

Holmes near Raleigh and volunteered for Co. B., 4th Infantry Battalion, NC Jr. Reserves, a battalion created from Alamance and Forsyth Counties. The commanding officers were Capt. A.L. Lancaster, Frst. Lt. A.M. Craig, Sec. Lt. William May, and Sec. Lt. C.B. Pfohl (of Salem). John served guard and picket duty in the eastern part of North Carolina—primarily at Sugar Loaf on the Cape Fear River near Fort Fisher. After his capture, he was transported to Point Lookout, where he remained until his release on June 20, 1865. On January 15, 1868, he married Mary Frances Eaton, the daughter of John Henry and Sara Elvina Kreeger Eaton. The two had nine children, and are buried at the Mt. Pleasant Methodist Church Cemetery in Tobaccoville. (SBR.)

16] PLEASANT HENDERSON HANES

Pleasant Henderson Hanes (October 16, 1845–June 9, 1925) was born to Alexander Martin and Jane March Hanes. When he was 19, Pleasant joined Co. E, 16th NC Battalion, of Gen. Fitzhugh Lee's division. Pleasant's two older brothers—Jacob H. and George A. Hanes—also joined in the Confederate cause, but did not survive. At the close of the war, Pleasant and three of his brothers (John, Phillip, and Benjamin) ventured into the business of manufacturing tobacco. In 1872, they built their first factory and began the B.F. Hanes Tobacco Company. On April 29, 1873, Pleasant married his cousin, Mary Lizora Fortune, the daughter of Charles Volney and Mary Margarette March Fortune. By 1889, after several mergers, the company, known as P.H. Hanes & Company, was the largest tobacco manufacturer in the area. In 1900, Pleasant sold his company to R.J. Reynolds for approximately $1 million. Eager for a new challenge, he organized the P.H. Hanes Knitting Company and the Hanes Hosiery Mill. In 1965, these two companies merged under the Hanes Corporation. Pleasant died on June 9, 1925, in Winston-Salem. He is shown here with his grandchildren—Jarvis Aubrey is on his lap, and the others are, from left to right, Newton, Huber Jr., Rosalie, Tol Old, and William Marvin. (HH.)

Four

FROM PLOW-BOYS
TO SOLDIERS:
THE SACRIFICE OF LIFE OR LIMB

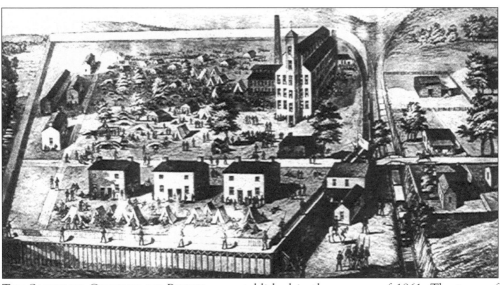

THE SALISBURY CONFEDERATE PRISON was established in the summer of 1861. The town of Salisbury was a major railroad link, as it was the largest town in western North Carolina during the Civil War. Imprisoned here initially were those who were referred to as "State Prisoners," i.e., Southern Union supporters, captured naval officers, and deserters from the Union, who were possibly spies. After the First Battle of Manassas (Bull Run), prisoners streamed into what was once a very quiet township. By 1864, in just six months time, thousands of Union prisoners were crammed into space adequate for only a thousand. Starvation and disease quickly increased the death count. In 1998, the Robert F. Hoke Chapter of the United Daughters of the Confederacy in Rowan County hosted the Salisbury Confederate Prison Symposium. Descendants of both Confederate and Union veterans shared documents, diaries, and letters of theirs ancestors who were in some way associated with the prison. Thermal imaging expert Mr. Bob Melia presented the findings of his four days of studying the prison site and recording thermal images from a helicopter. He found the prison site to be much larger than previously believed. He also concurred with historian Louis Brown, who concluded that about 4,000 Union prisoners died at the prison, despite federal government figures of 11,700. (NCR.)

1] ALFRED H. BAIRD

2] JAMES B. GORDON

3] J.L. SCHAUB

1] ALFRED H. BAIRD

Alfred H. Baird volunteered with the 1st Regiment of North Carolina, which had been organized for state service for six months. Initially he was made color sergeant under the command of Col. (later Gen.) Daniel Harvey Hill. Alfred's regiment traveled to Yorktown, arriving there on June 9, 1861. He was detailed with about 25 men who "drove in the Federal pickets in front of Fortress Monroe, capturing one of their men—the first prisoner of war." It was during this battle at Bethel, Virginia, that the first Confederate soldier was killed. In a letter to his sister, Alfred shared the following:

> [Col. Palmer] informed me that there were three companies of North Carolina cavalry at Big Creek Gap, and he desired to form a battalion; and, as a result, I was commissioned major of the battalion. This occurred before I was 18 years old. Col. Scott commanded our brigade up to the time of the battle of Chickamauga. My battalion (the 5th NC) had been in active service all the time, and I had lost about half of my men. After the battle, we were consolidated with the 7th NC Battalion (commanded by Lt.-Col. G.N. Folk), and formed the 6th NC Regiment of Cavalry. I was commissioned lieutenant-colonel of the regiment, with Folk colonel and John I. Spann major . . . I have never heard of an officer of the same rank younger than myself. I was lieutenant-colonel at 19, commanding a regiment. I will let others tell how I earned the promotions. I will only say that I was in the first fight on land and I think the last, and I always tried to do my duty. I served under Morgan, Forrest, Pegram and Hampton. (CVM.)

2] JAMES B. GORDON

James B. Gordon (November 2, 1822–May 18, 1864) was born in Wilkes County. During his childhood he attended the school of Peter Ney in Iredell County, and he later studied at Emory and Henry College, Virginia. In his local community he was a political leader and ran a successful mercantile business. When the call for troops came, he enlisted in the Wilkes Guards, 1st Cavalry Regiment, NC State Troops. James served as the lieutenant, captain, and major of this regiment, which was assigned to the brigade of Gen. J.E.B. Stuart. In September 1863, he attained the rank of brigadier general and was assigned to command the NC Cavalry Brigade. He fought gallantly throughout the war, leadinghis men through countless battles. During the battle to save Richmond, he was mortally wounded, and he died on May 18, 1864. In 1898, James B. Gordon was posthumously honored when the United Daughters of the Confederacy of Forsyth County named their chapter after him.

3] J.L. SCHAUB

J.L. Schaub, seen here as a young and older man, was born on January 9, 1843, in Davidson County. His mother was Amanda Lambeth, the daughter of Dr. Shadrick Lambeth. When about 15 years of age, J.L. attended the Blair Academy at Thomasville, as well as the Yadkin Institute. When the Civil War commenced, he returned home from the institute, and joined the Thomasville Rifles, reorganized under Capt. Willis L. Miller. Eventually this company became a part of the 4th NC Infantry, with Junius Daniel as colonel. Owing to the enlistment of ten regiments as regulars, the 4th NC Infantry was changed to the 14th Regiment. Corporal Schaub experienced battle at Yorktown, Seven Pines, Mechanicsville, Cold Harbor, Gaines's Mill, and Malvern Hill. He also fought in the Battles of Boonesboro, Sharpsburg, and Fredricksburg. (AMVR.)

4] ALEXANDER WESLEY PALMER

Alexander Wesley Palmer (May 31, 1840–April 25, 1907), the son of German-native Orren A. Palmer, was assigned to Co. D, NC 3rd Cavalry (41st Regiment), but no other military information is known about him. On January 31, 1866, he married Virginia Victoria Rives, the daughter of William Alston and Lydia McBryde Reid Rives, and the couple had eight children. The Palmer family does not appear in the Forsyth County census records until 1900. During this time period they were living on West End Boulevard in Winston. Alexander died in Forsyth Country, and is buried in the Bethlehem Methodist Church in Sanford. His tombstone simply says "A Civil War Soldier." (OP.)

5] PHILLIP NORMAN WHITMAN JR.

Phillip Norman Whitman Jr. was born on November 26, 1831, to Philip Sr. (1787–1860) and Mary Johnson Whitman (1792–1872), who lived in the Clemmons area of Forsyth County. On February 18, 1857, he married Amanda Caroline Jones (September 17, 1831–March 4, 1911), the daughter of Wylie (1798–1861) and Maria Magdalena Hauser Jones (1804–1891). Phillip Jr. was a prosperous farmer in western Forsyth County. He served as a private with Co. G, 7th Regiment, Confederate Cavalry. In the 1870 Forsyth County Census, he is listed with his wife and their four children: Mary, Leonora, Martha V., and William. Shown here are the following, from left to right: (front row) Phillip Jr. and his wife, Amanda; (back row) Mary Ida Whitman and Martha Virginia Whitman. (PJT.)

6] THE 65TH REGIMENT, NC CAVALRY

The 65th Regiment, 6th NC Cavalry, poses for a photograph. They are as follows: (bottom) Sec. Lt. Wiley P. Thomas, Co. A; (lower left) Capt. William B. Councill, Co. B; (lower right) Sec. Lt. Stephen J. Brown, Co. A; (middle) Col. George Nathaniel Folk; (top) Capt. V.S. Lask, Co. I (formerly the 5th Battalion); (top left) Capt. and AQM Martin V. Moor; (top right) Capt. Barton Robey Brown, Co. A. Captain Lask was a prisoner on Johnson's Island from 1863 to 1865.

4] ALEXANDER WESLEY PALMER

5] PHILLIP NORMAN WHITMAN JR.
AND MEMBERS OF HIS FAMILY

6] THE 65TH REGIMENT, NC CAVALRY

7] JAMES POLK COVINGTON

8] RUFUS CALVIN HAMBY

9] SAMUEL FORKNER

10] WILLIAM ALEXANDER BRAY

11] MICHAEL ALEXANDER SAPP

7] JAMES POLK COVINGTON

James Polk Covington (September 12, 1845–May 6, 1922) was born in Rockingham County to John Anderson and Sarah Pulliam Covington. Sometime during or just after the Civil War, the Covington family moved from Rockingham County to Stokes County, where they resided for the remainder of their lives. James enlisted in the Confederate Army at Camp Holmes on May 27, 1864, when he was 18 years old. He was one of the gallant young men who served with Co. C, 3rd Regiment, Jr. Reserves, also known as "the Boys of 65." Most of these soldiers were from Stokes and Person Counties. This regiment was a consolidation of the 4th, 7th, and 8th Battalions. The NC Jr. Reserves were under the exclusive control of the state governor. Under Confederate and state law, the reserves were not required to cross the state line to engage in battles. This regiment is famous for its determined defense of Fort Fisher, which was strategically located on a point of a narrow peninsula between the ocean and Cape Fear River. James and his comrades were as determined to keep the fort for the Confederacy as the Yankees were to capture it. He showed the same dedication of service that he exhibited during the war throughout his life and worked hard to improve his community by supporting education. For several years he served in the public office of surveyor of Stokes County and as a justice of the peace. He was instrumental in organizing the Brown Mountain Baptist Church and the Brims Grove Baptist Church. James married Mary Jane Gibson on January 10, 1871, in Stokes County. They had six children: Louella V., Lilla C., Joseph Anderson, Mary M., Edgar Alphonsa, and Thomas Jefferson. James is buried at Brims Grove Baptist Church in Stokes County. (SCT.)

8] RUFUS CALVIN HAMBY

Rufus Calvin Hamby was born on March 5, 1833, to Ephraim and Elizabeth Money Hamby. He enlisted in Rowan County on April 1, 1862. The following September, he was detailed as a gunsmith at Petersburg, Virginia. He rejoined his company two years later in September 1864. At the time of his parole on May 3, 1865, Rufus was a prisoner of war. His first wife was Nancy Swink from Rowan County; he later remarried to Carolina Young. From his marriages he had the following children: Lee (who became a doctor), Lock, Frank, Laura, Maggie, Michael, and John Hamby. (HBJ.)

9] SAMUEL FORKNER

Samuel Forkner was the son of James and Mary Harris Forkner. Military records indicate that he enlisted on September 5, 1862, with Co. A, 2nd Regiment, NC Infantry. He was later captured and imprisoned at Point Lookout. After his release, he remained in the hospital in Richmond. Samuel and his wife, Anna Wade Forkner, had the following children: Mildred, Deborah, Lucy, Robert, David, Kate, Alice, and Dalton. (HBJ.)

10] William Alexander Bray

William Alexander Bray (*c.* 1834–July 1863) was born in Surry County to Henry C. and Martha M. Poindexter Bray. He married Martha Mahala Poindexter, the daughter of Archibald Tyrell Poindexter and Matilda Overby Poindexter. On August 10, 1861, William volunteered in Dobson with Co. B, 2nd Battalion, and was elected to sergeant the same day. In February 1862, his battalion was captured at Roanoke Island. They were paroled at Elizabeth City on February 21, 1862, and exchanged on August 18, 1862. The battalion was reorganized on September 25, 1862. William was promoted to second lieutenant on December 17, 1862. He was killed during the Battle of Gettysburg in July 1863. Sometime after the war, his remains were exhumed from the battlefield and relocated to the Confederate Section, Grave No. 512, Oakwood Cemetery, Raleigh. In this photograph, he is holding a wooden pistol, which was commonly used as a prop for many military photographs. In a letter to his wife, William shared his loneliness:

> "*Camp B 2nd Batt, Camp near Kinston NC, 1 Mar 1863 Dear Wife, I take the oportunlty [sic] of writing you a few lines. I am not very well I have a pain in my Side but nothing Serious I hope . . . I think it very strange that I never get any letters from you all the rest gets letters every week. Seems I never hear a word from you except if Somebody comes from there. It looks like if you wrote much, Some of the letters would surely get here. If you knew how bad I wanted to hear from you and my sweet little children you would write a many a letter to me since I want to see you the worst in the world. I would give any thing in this world to be at home with you and them little babies tonight, bless their little bodies. How bad I want to see them I have forgot how they look but I hope I will live to see you all again but that is uncertain for we are engaged in a uncertain business. I thought Some time ago that the war would Soon end but I see no prospect of its ending now. The Yankees will Soon have three million more men in the field and time alone can only tell how the war will end. I Shall try to get to come home this Spring or Summer if I live and get the chance. You have no idie how bad I want to see you and the children, but you know it is impossible for me to get to come home, this war, this awful war. When will it end. Never till every thing is ruined I fear. Write quickly and often be sure to write as soon as you get this letter. Tell me a heap about Tom and Susa. Tell them to be good children, maby papa will come home. Sometimes I grives [to] live to come home. You must do the best you can, but I hope the god that rules all things will spare my life to come home again. It looks like I would give any thing if I could be at home only two days. Orders have come at this moment for us to be ready to march at Six o'clock in the morning. It is now ten o'clock at night and we are all fixing to start. I will write again soon as I can. Your husband till death. W.A. Bray PS. Write two three letters as quick as you get this so I will be sure to get one. it seems like I cannot write enough.*" (JSC.)

11] Michael Alexander Sapp

Michael Alexander Sapp (August 8, 1840–May 20, 1900) was born in Forsyth County. On March 18, 1862, at the age of 21, Michael joined the 52nd Regiment, NC Infantry. He was wounded in Goldsboro on December 17, 1862, and returned to duty prior to March 1, 1863. On October 14, 1863, he was captured at Bristoe Station, Virginia, and was confined at the Old

12] DANIEL AND SUSANNAH NORMAN BARKER

Capitol Prison in Washington, D.C., until his transfer on October 27, 1863, to Point Lookout. On February 2, 1864, he deserted the Confederate Army, signed the Oath of Allegiance, and joined Co. G, 1st Regiment, U.S. Volunteer Infantry. He is buried in the Mt. Tabor Cemetery in Winston-Salem. (TC.)

12] DANIEL AND SUSANNAH NORMAN BARKER

Daniel Barker (March 18, 1835–December 19, 1910), the son of Jeremiah and Susannah Galysan Barker, was born in Surry Co. On April 18, 1852, he married Susannah Norman. He enlisted in the Confederate Army on August 17, 1862, in Wake Co. with Co. I, 18th NC Infantry. According to military records, the 18th Regiment was at Sharpsburg or near Harpers Ferry where they were joined by "a large number of raw recruits from North Carolina . . . that . . . have been supplied with guns." The division moved from the Sharpsburg area to the area of Winchester and Charlestown, Virginia, where some of the men came down with typhoid fever, measles, and pneumonia. Around May 3, 1863, during the Battle of Chancellorsville, Daniel was injured by an exploding shell. After a sick furlough, he rejoined his regiment sometime between September 1863 and February 1864. Records list him as being at Appomattox Court House at the time of the Confederate surrender. The following is an article about Daniel written in the *Greensboro Record* newspaper and recorded in the *Yadkin Valley News* on October 16, 1891:

> "On 23rd of Mar. last a party of raiders under Deputy Collector Bascomb Fields had been fired upon in Surry . . . R.I. Barnwell, of Hendersonville, was killed and Brim

was seriously wounded . . . detectives sent to Surry . . . Barker was arrested, tried and set free by jury on Aug. last . . . He was 3 years in the Confederate service . . . . made a good soldier . . . but received a shock to his brain from a bursting shell at the Battle of Chancellorsville where fell the gallant Stonewall Jackson in whose command he was . . . from which he has never fully recovered."

Family members say Daniel and Susannah are buried in the Barker family cemetery in Round Peak. Although the exact location of their burial plots is unknown, a Civil War headstone has been erected for Daniel. (WH.)

13] SPENCER JOSEPH HANES

Spencer Joseph Hanes (May 18, 1837–April 9, 1879) was born to Alexander M. and Jane March Hanes, and was educated in Germanton. During the war, he served as captain of Co. E, 42nd NC Infantry. In July 1864, during a battle near Petersburg, he received wounds so severe that he lay near death. His mother traveled to Virginia to care for him, eventually bringing him home to Fulton in Davie County. In a letter home, Spencer's condition was described as follows:

> There was an operation performed upon his shoulder. The Dr. trimmed the gangrenish flesh with a red hot knife and seared it with a red hot iron. Mother wrote that she had never seen anything equal to it. She said the Dr. was going to take him to the Danville Hospital, as he thinks there is a great danger of him taking 'irisilplus.' " Spencer survived his injuries, however, and on Sept. 19, 1865, he married Mary Jane Clement, the daughter of Godfrey and Elizabeth Buckner (Brown) Clement. He died 13 years later at his home in Fulton, and is buried in the M.E. Church Cemetery in that same town. His obituary described him as a "gallant soldier of the Confederacy. (FBH.)

14] SAMUEL JEFFERSON LAMBETH

Samuel Jefferson Lambeth, the last surviving Confederate veteran of Davidson County, passed away in the home of his daughter, Mrs. Hattie Lambeth Tesh, on June 17, 1940. He was born on April 1, 1846, in Davidson County to Samuel J. and Rachel Myers Lambeth, whose families were among the original settlers to the area from Indiana. He married Miss Barbara Miller of Davidson. During the war, he was a member of the Jr. Reserve, and was stationed in the eastern part of the state. He was a longtime member of the A.A. Hill Camp of United Confederate Veterans, which ceased to exist after his death, as he was its last member. He was a little over 94 years old when he died. At the time of his death, there were only 31 Confederate veterans still living in North Carolina. (ETB.)

13] SPENCER JOSEPH HANES

14] SAMUEL JEFFERSON LAMBETH

15] ROMULUS BRADBERRY TESH

16] JOHN WALKER BITTING   17] RICHARD LOYSTON YARBROUGH

18] MEMBERS OF THE 22ND REGIMENT   19] THE 22ND NC INFANTRY

15] ROMULUS BRADBERRY TESH

Romulus Bradberry Tesh (February 15, 1840–November 11, 1919) was born to David and Rachael Morris Tesh. At the time of his enlistment on August 8, 1862, with Co. K, 48th NC Infantry, Romulus was a simple farmer in Davidson County. During the Battle of Fredericksburg (December 13, 1862), Tesh sustained an injury to his left shoulder. He was reported as absent-wounded on the rolls of January-June and September-October, 1863, and the January-April 1864 muster rolls reported him absent without leave. He was officially paroled at Greensboro on or about May 5, 1865. He married Christina Abigail "Abby" Green (May 8, 1847–July 31, 1917), the daughter of Joseph Green and Christina Motsinger Green. Romulus and Abby are buried at the Clemmons Baptist Church Cemetery in Clemmons. (PJT.)

16] JOHN WALKER BITTING

John Walker Bitting (February 1843–May 1910) was born at Tom's Creek, Surry County, to Walter Raleigh Bitting and Susan Rebeccah Hampton Bitting. John was the brother-in-law of Joseph Anthony Bitting and Louise Wilson Bitting. On March 25, 1862, at the age of 18, he enlisted with the 48th NC Infantry, serving as a sharpshooter in Walker's Brigade, Hill's Division. He was promoted to captain of his company after the Battle of Bristol Station, Virginia. In this battle, the company captain and all the lieutenants were killed and John himself was severely wounded. In his four years of service, he participated in 25 battles and skirmishes. In December 1862, he was wounded in his left hip at Fredricksburg. After returning to duty, he was wounded again, this time at Bristol Station on October 14, 1863. Records show he was also hospitalized in Richmond on May 15, 1864. He resigned from service on February 24, 1865. His official United States pardon was printed in the 13th edition of the *People's Press* in 1865. After the war he married Miss Julia Elizabeth Wilson and engaged in the mercantile business, first in Salisbury, North Carolina, and then in Manor, Travis County, Texas, where he ran a large cotton business. Julia died before January 1899. In her will she left all of her holdings to John, except for what was delegated to her children. John died in Manor in May 1910, leaving behind a second wife and three daughters. (CVM.)

17] RICHARD LOYSTON YARBROUGH

Richard Loyston Yarbrough (1833–1908) was born in Caswell County to Joseph Yarbrough Jr. and Mary Herring Yarbrough. He enlisted as a private with Co. B., 59th Regiment, NC Infantry (the nickname for the 4th NC Cavalry). His brother, John B., fought with Co. C, 13th Regiment, NC Infantry. Richard married Rachel Pass and relocated to Forsyth County in 1879. The two purchased 300 acres (at $3 per acre) of property that adjoined the Conrad property east of Muddy Creek, between Bethania and Bethabara. Richard was a millwright by trade, but he also constructed gristmills and worked as a carpenter, brick layer, and farmer. One of the first people to welcome him and his wife into the community was Mr. Francis Pratt (Co. K., 52nd NC Infantry). Richard died in Forsyth County and is buried at the New Hope Methodist Church Cemetery in Winston-Salem. (HY.)

18] Members of the 22nd Regiment

These members of the 22nd Regiment, from left to right, are as follows: (bottom) Pvt. William T. Abernathy and Pvt. Aurelius J. Dula; (middle) Frst. Lt. J.B. Clarke; (top) Ensign Sion H. Oxford and Pvt. S.F. Harper. (NCR.)

19] The 22nd NC Infantry

The 22nd NC Infantry was organized near Raleigh in July 1861. Originally called the 12th Volunteers, it had members from Caldwell, McDowell, Guilford, Alleghany, Caswell, Stokes, and Randolph Counties. Shown here are the following, from left to right: (bottom) Sec. Lt. W.W. Dickson and Sec. Lt. and Drill Master Walter Clark; (middle) Col. Johnston J. Pettigrew; (top) Capt. Thomas D. Jones and Frst. Lt. and Adjt. Graham Daves. (NCR.)

20] William Henry Roberson

William Henry Roberson (May 19, 1844–August 10, 1922) enlisted at Camp Vance on June 12, 1864, and joined Co. B., 22nd Regiment, NC Infantry. He was captured at Hatcher's Run, Virginia, on April 2, 1865, and confined to Hart's Island, in New York Harbor, which he described as nothing but a "concentration camp." He was released on or about June 19, 1865, after taking the Oath of Allegiance. On November 26, 1867, he married Elizabeth Hester (October 4, 1844–September 12, 1909) of Forsyth County, the daughter of Moses and Matilda Barham Hester. William's application for military pension, filed May 20, 1902, described his poor health. The doctor's examination reported that William suffered from deafness, impaired vision, and a severe cough from chronic bronchitis, caused by exposure to measles while in military service. As an old man, he would recount stories of his experiences in the Civil War to his grandchildren. One day, while telling stories on his front porch, he angrily said, "If I thought I had one ounce of Yankee blood in my veins, I would take and knife and cut it out!" William and Elizabeth are buried at Loves Methodist Church Cemetery in Walkertown, Forsyth County. (PRH.)

21] Martin Franklin "Francis" Gough

Martin Franklin "Francis" Gough (May 15, 1844–January 12, 1930) was born in Surry County to Henry Milton and Mary Allen Gough. On June 18, 1861, in East Bend, Francis joined Co. F, 28th NC Infantry, as a private. Wounded at Gettysburg, he was placed in the Chimborazo Hospital #5 in Richmond. The injuries to his legs required him to rely on two canes for the rest of his life. He was present or accounted for through February 1865 and was discharged in Greensboro. He married Dicey Rosannah "Rosa" Williams (1854–1881) on September 5, 1869, in Yadkin County. The couple had seven children. After Rosa's death, Francis married again, this time to Rebecca Permelia Caudle. He was the father of 11 children by the time he died at the age of 85 in Boonville. (JCS.)

20] William Henry Roberson

21] Martin Franklin "Francis" Gough

22] James M. Starling

23] William Addison Tesh

22] James M. Starling

James M. Starling enlisted on June 18, 1861, in East Bend. Throughout the war he served with Co. F, 28th NC Infantry. The Yadkin Boys were a part of Branch's Brigade in A.P. Hill's division. James mustered in as private and promoted to sergeant in 1862. Official records reported him as "absent—sent to hospital wounded" in November-December 1862. The place and date of where his injuries occurred is unknown, but records indicate he was a patient in Hospital #22 in December of 1862, after the Battle of Fredericksburg. His next promotion was to third lieutenant on May 11, 1863, a rank he held until the end of the war. At the Battle of Spotsylvania, Lieutenant Starling was among several men captured in an attempt to take an enemy battery. He was later rescued by his own men, who overtook his Union captors. In a report to Capt. E.J. Hale dated July 19, 1864, Col. W.H.A. Speer duly noted James's bravery during the Spotsylvania battle. According to muster rolls for September, October, November, and December 1864, he commanded Company F in the absence of higher ranking officers who were at that time commanding the 28th Regiment. He was present or accounted for through March 14, 1865. The records indicate he was "Granted Leave S.O. #66/11 Dept & Army NC VA Lee." After the war, James married Virginia E. Poindexter on Jan. 27, 1869, in Yadkin County. They lived and farmed in Surry County along the Yadkin River. On July 6, 1877, at the age of 38, he died, reportedly from old war wounds. Surviving him were his wife and four small children, the last of which was born one month after James's death. (TLSS.)

23] William Addison Tesh

William Addison Tesh (October 12, 1843–May 4, 1864) was born to Moses and Mary "Mollie" Mock Tesh. He was a descendant of Heinrich Tesch, who settled in northern Rowan County in 1771. On March 8, 1862, William enlisted with Co. I, 28th Regiment, NC Infantry. At the time he was living with his family in the Little Yadkin district of Forsyth County, where his father worked as a blacksmith. In October, his regiment camped near Winchester, Virginia. In a letter home, he tells his family that his uncle, John Mock, is dead, and then goes on to describe the fighting:

> ". . . I have bin in all the Fights the regiment has bin in and thats 15 and I have come through safe. We had a Fight at Harpers Ferry and Taken ten Thousand prisoners and ten thousand stands arms and 60 pieces artilery and all their Commisary stores and every thing they had and then paroled them and sent them home and then we left and Went over in Maryland and had a fight at Sharpsburg and got our General Branch Killed . . . and then we Fell Back across the potomac and then we got in a Fight at Sheppardstown and runn them in the river and then we had our Funn a killing them as they Crossed the river. I tell you we saw hard times. Some times we would have to do with out rations 2 days at a time and marched all day and mabe half the night and then start next morning By day light. I tell you that tries a Fellows spunk certain."

By December 1862, William longed to be home for Christmas:

> ". . . I would give Fifty Dollars For a Furlow For Thirty days Just to be at home at Christmas to get something good to Eat . . . we havent got no tents only two in the company. I have got my Blanket stretched and it is raining and snowing . . ."

24] MEMBERS OF THE 32ND REGIMENT

25] LEMUEL ALBERTY

William faithfully continued his correspondence with his family until his death in Lynchburg, Virginia. He wrote 74 letters between March 1862 and May 1864; they are presently in the Special Collections Library of Duke University, Durham, North Carolina. (PJT.)

24] MEMBERS OF THE 32ND REGIMENT

Members of the 32nd Regiment pose for a photographer. They are, from left to right, as follows: (bottom) Corp. Augustus Little and Courier H.A. London; (middle) Col. E.C. Brabble; (top) Surg. William H. Battle and Capt. W.I. London. (NCR.)

25] LEMUEL ALBERTY

Lemuel Alberty (May 11, 1842–May 5, 1915) was born to Nathaniel and Rebecca Bray Alberty of Surry County. Nathaniel was a preacher of the Primitive Baptist Church of the Pigeon Roost Creek area. Like many of the young men in his township, Lemuel volunteered on March 18, 1862, to serve with Co. A, 28th Regiment, NC Infantry. At the time of his enlistment, he received a bounty of $50, which was a good sum at that time. He stayed in good health until June 1864, when he was hospitalized for pneumonia. In August 1864, probably while on furlough, he married Lucinda White. They eventually raised a family of six children. After the war, Lemuel served his community as a deacon at the Center Primitive Baptist

26] WILLIAM WASHINGTON KAPP

27] OLIVER J. LEHMAN

28] DR. SYLVANUS DAVID AND JANE TRANSOU DAVIS

Church. In 1913, on his 71st birthday, he and several of his old comrades reminisced about their military struggles. Lemuel died on May 5, 1915; Lucinda died in 1923. The two are buried in the Liberty Primitive Baptist Church in Surry County. (HBJ.)

26] WILLIAM WASHINGTON KAPP

William Washington Kapp (December 28, 1840–February 7, 1934) volunteered for service with Co. K, 28th NC Infantry, enlisting at Bethania. His father, Alexander Sanders Kapp, also served during the War between the States as a member of Co. H., 74th Regiment, NC Infantry. In March of 1862, William was imprisoned for two months at Hart's Island, eventually being paroled in July of 1865. In 1927, he applied for and was approved for a pension for his military services. That same year, on May 10, he attended the Confederate Veterans Memorial Service held in Winston-Salem. His Confederate service was listed in his obituary:

> "William Washington Kapp, 93, died at the home of his daughter, Mrs. A.E. Stanley, Efird Street, Montview, this morning at 4 o'clock. Mr. Kapp had been in declining health for the past three years, but his final illness came with an attack of pneumonia about two weeks ago. He was born near Rural Hall, Dec. 28, 1840, and he spent his entire life in the county, a successful farmer, retiring sometime ago. He was a Confederate veteran, serving during the War Between the States as a member of the 28th Regiment, CSA. Volunteering at the beginning of the war, he served during the entire struggle." (JDB.)

27] OLIVER J. LEHMAN

Oliver J. Lehman was born to Eugene C. (d. 1857) and Amanda Butner Lehman (d. 1868). The Lehman and Butner Store was established in 1836 by Eugene and his father-in-law, H.H. Butner. The store benefitted greatly from the stage route from Salem to Bethania. Eugene died in Baltimore in March of 1857 while traveling north to purchase goods for his mercantile business. When Oliver joined the Confederate Army he organized the band of the 33rd Regiment, NC State Troops. Most likely he enlisted in Hyde County, as did many of his neighbors. Many of the members of the 33rd Regimental Band were citizens of Bethania. Those enlisting in Pfafftown during July and August 1861 were W.W. Anderson, William N. Butner, James H. Conrad, Edwin C. Dull, C.H. Fulk, Lewis A. Hartman, P.T. Lehman, Julius F. Stauber, and Levin J. Stroupe. Oliver eventually married Eliza Jane Doub, the daughter of John Wesley Doub and Elizabeth Dull, and the couple had several children: Lillian Lehman (1867–1943) married Edward F. Strickland (1863–1951); Ella Lehman (1877–1941) married L.G. Barlow; Bessie Lehman (1880–1954) married John Walter Daniel (1864–1954); and Eugene W. Lehman (1872–1937) married Elizabeth Transou (1879–1958), the daughter of Rufus Edward Transou and Frances Augusta Grabs. (NCR.)

28] Dr. Sylvanus David and Jane Transou Davis

Dr. Sylvanus David Davis was born in Surry County on September 8, 1832. In 1857, he started his medical practice while living in the Bethania home of A.C. Transou. In 1861, he married Jane Transou, the daughter of Ephriam and Adalaid Cooper Transou. Sylvanus enlisted as a private on July 15, 1862, with Co. H, 33rd NC Infantry. He served with this unit until the surrender of the Confederacy. He was promoted to hospital steward in July 1863, and later transferred to field and staff. After the war, he returned to his medical practice in Pfafftown. His wife had four brothers and at least one uncle who served in the Confederate Army. Her uncle, J.A. (Julius) Transou, served with the 26th Regimental Band. Her four brothers were Charles E. Transou (26th Regiment Band), Lewis B. Transou (Co. D, 57th Regiment, NC Troops), Ruben P. Transou (Co. K, 21st Regiment, NC Troops), and Owen C. Transou (Company K, 21st Regiment, NC Troops). (HY.)

29] Joseph B. Siewers

Joseph B. Siewers was a resident of Forsyth County when the war started. As did many of the men in the community of Bethania, he originally signed up in Hyde County with the 33rd NC Regiment. His father, Jacob Siewers, was the pastor of the Bethania Moravian Church, and made no secret of his support of Unionism. Joseph was present or accounted for until his capture at Gettysburg in July of 1863. Less than a month after his imprisonment at Fort Delaware, he signed the Oath of Allegiance. On August 1, 1863, he joined the Federals and was assigned to Ah'ls Independent Co., Delaware, Heavy Artillery.

30] Jonathon Edwin Speace (Speas)

Jonathan Edwin Speace (Speas) (August 1, 1840–July 5, 1864) was born in Old Richmond Township, in what is now Forsyth County, to Jonathan and Nancy Waller Speas [sic]. He married 21-year-old Lydia Adelaide Hauser, the daughter of Isaac and Drucilla Kerby Hauser, on January 16, 1859, in Forsyth County. To their marriage were born four children. Jonathan enlisted twice during the Civil War. On July 15, 1862, he enlisted as a private of Co. H., 33rd NC Infantry. He was present or accounted for until his capture at Chancellorsville on May 5, 1863. After being sent to Washington, D.C., he was eventually paroled and transferred to City Point, Virginia, to be exchanged on May 13, 1863. Muster rolls list him absent without leave on June 1, 1863, returning to duty on March 6, 1864. It was during this time period he was captured at or near Wilderness, Virginia. He was confined at Point Lookout, and on May 30, 1864, while in prison, he deserted the Confederate Army and joined the Federals—an action that caused his father to disinherit him. Jonathan was assigned to Co. I, 1st Regiment, US Volunteer Infantry, but was soon hospitalized in Hampton, Virginia, where he died July 5, 1864. His grave site is No. 3873 in the National Cemetery in Hampton, and he is listed on the U.S. Roll of Honor. His last child, Wiley Edwin Speas [sic], was born in Norfolk, Virginia, on October 25, 1864, approximately three months after Jonathan's death. The United States awarded his widow a pension of $8 per month. She also received an additional $2 per month for each of her children under the age of 16. The pension began on July 8, 1864, and continued through her widowhood. (JSB.)

29] JOSEPH B. SIEWERS

30] JONATHON EDWIN SPEACE (SPEAS)

31] RUFUS AUSTIN JARRELL AND FAMILY

31] RUFUS AUSTIN JARRELL AND FAMILY

Rufus Austin Jarrell (September 15, 1839–March 31, 1921), the son of Fountain and Fannie Jarrell, was born in Rockingham County. Prior to the war he resided in Surry County and earned a living as a farmer. He enlisted in the Confederate Army on March 18, 1862, at the age of 22, becoming a private with Co. A, 28th NC Infantry. Rufus suffered a wound in the left leg at Ox Hill, Virginia, on September 1, 1862. He was listed as absent-sick until October 1862. The January–February 1863 rolls list him as a deserter, but he eventually returned to his regiment, and was wounded in the left eye and in both arms while in Jericho Mills, Virginia, on May 23, 1864. He returned from sick furlough in November-December 1864. Around February 24, 1865, he was captured and imprisoned in Washington, D.C. During his imprisonment he officially deserted the Confederate Army and signed the Oath of Allegiance. On October 6, 1868, Rufus married Susan Sandifer, the daughter of Perm and Martha Sandifer. They had two children, Charlie Anthony and Benjamin Franklin Jarrell. Rufus married a second time, to Susan Turney, the daughter of Vincent and Polly Spencer Turney. He died in the Round Peak section of Surry County, and is buried in the old Jarrell Cemetery off the Dan Calloway Road with his first wife buried on his left side and his second wife buried on his right. Shown here, from left to right, are Susan Turney Jarrell, Benjamin Franklin Jarrell, Rufus Austin Jarrell, and Charles Anthony Jarrell, c. 1895. (WH.)

32] MEMBERS OF THE 35TH NC INFANTRY

Members of the 35th NC Infantry pose for a photograph. They are, from left to right, as follows: (bottom row) Capt. David G. Maxwell, Capt. P.J. Johnson, and Frst. Lt. and Adjutant Walter Clark; (middle row) Lt. Col. Simon B. Taylor and Capt. Wm. H.S. Burgwyn; (top row) Col. M.W. Ransom, Col. John G. Jones, and Col. J.T. Johnson. Captain Ransom later served as brigadier general of five different regiments: the 24th, 25th, 35th, 49th, and 56th. (NCR.)

33] ROMULUS LEEDY COX

Romulus Leedy Cox was born in Forsyth County. A well-respected teacher before the war, Romulus began his military service in April of 1862, at the age of 27. Not long after his appointment as second lieutenant in Co. K, 52nd NC Infantry, he received another promotion, to first lieutenant, about July 1, 1863. During the Battle of Globe Tavern he sustained injuries in the bottom of his foot and was hospitalized at Richmond. He received a medical furlough through December of 1864. In March of 1865, he received another medical furlough, for "nephritis." He was at his home in Forsyth County at the time of Lee's surrender at Appomattox. On December 16, 1927, his two daughters, Miss Bettie Cox (b. May 10, 1873) and Miss Daisy Cox (b. December 4, 1877), joined the James B. Gordon Chapter of the United Daughters of the Confederacy, registering their membership through their father's service.

32] MEMBERS OF THE 35TH NC INFANTRY

33] ROMULUS LEEDY COX

34] FRANCIS MARION AND SARAH M. AXOM PRATT

35] John William Beck and Family

36] The Wall Brothers

34] FRANCIS MARION AND SARAH M. AXOM PRATT

Francis Marion Pratt (February 10, 1836–January 6, 1918) and Sarah M. Axom Pratt pose for a photographer. Francis was born in Bethabara to William Gholson and Johanna Elizabeth Butner Pratt. He was one of eight children; the others were John Lewis (Co. K, 21st Regiment, NC Infantry), Mary Eliza, Emily C., Clarissa A., Robert W., Henry T., and Antoinette. He enlisted with Co. K, 52nd NC Infantry, on May 10, 1862, was captured during the Battle of Falling Waters, and was taken to Point Lookout. He was paroled on March 3, 1864, then exchanged at City Point, Virginia. Francis was then detailed with his division wagon train through December 1864. On April 9, 1865, he was present during the surrender at Appomattox. He returned home to Forsyth County on May 15, 1864, and on February 25, 1872, he married Sarah M. Axom in Surry County. The two had the following children: William, Laura Frances, T. Bernard, Eugene C., Edward P., Joseph Marion, Fannie E., Lelia G., Minnie Lize, and Lavora. Francis is buried at the New Hope Methodist Church. (HY.)

35] JOHN WILLIAM BECK AND FAMILY

John William Beck (February 14, 1835–February 14, 1916) enlisted with Co. K, 52nd NC Infantry, on March 10, 1864. He was present or accounted for until being captured at Stephenson's Depot at Winchester, Virginia, on July 20, 1864. He was initially confined at Camp Chase, Ohio, but was later transferred to Boulware's and Cox's Wharves on James River, where he was received for exchange on March 10–12, 1865. He died on his 81st birthday in Forsyth County. Shown here from left to right are Lucy Beck (daughter), John William Beck, Ruben Beck (son), Martha Jane Ziglar Beck (wife), and Susie Beck (daughter). (HY.)

36] THE WALL BROTHERS

The Wall Brothers, Pvt. William Andrew Watkins Wall (left), Pvt. John Richard Francis Wall (center), and Pvt. Drury Benjamin Wesley Wall (right), pose for a photographer. The members of the Wall family were originally natives of Virginia, but they had moved to Stokes County by the time the war started. All three brothers immediately volunteered with Co. D, 52nd Regiment, NC Infantry, McCulloch's Avengers, upon the outbreak of war. William enlisted on March 19, 1862. Records list him as absent without leave on July 1, 1862. Family records show that he died at home in Stokes County on September 25, 1862. It is believed that he was furloughed home due to disease. That particular summer, between April 19 and September 27, 1862, 78 members of the 52nd died of disease. Drury also enlisted on March 19, 1862. During the Picket-Pettigrew-Trimble Charge at Gettysburg, he sustained an injury that required the amputation of one of his legs. Taken as a prisoner of war on July 4, 1863, he was sent from Gettysburg to a Federal hospital. His final destination was Point Lookout, where he remained until his exchange on March 20, 1864. Drury received a furlough home on May 21, 1864, where he died shortly after his arrival. John Richard Francis, also part of the Picket-Pettigrew-Trimble Charge, fought along side his brother at Gettysburg. His next battle was on July 14, 1863, at Falling Waters, Maryland. Pettigrew's brigade had been assigned the responsibility of protecting the rear of the Army of Northern Virginia. Taking an opportunity to rest his men, Pettigrew chose a wooded hillside by the roadside located between 1 and 2 miles from the river at Williamsport. His cavalry passed on for the purpose of crossing the river. Not long after, another body of cavalry suddenly advanced upon them. Some of the superior officers, mistaking the men as their own, ordered the soldiers not to fire. The error of the order was quickly realized as the Yankee cavalry descended upon them. There was no opportunity for the 52nd regiment to gather themselves for defense. In just a matter of moments 71 men, including General Pettigrew, were either killed or wounded. John Richard Francis Wall was among the few prisoners taken to Point Lookout, where he eventually died, most likely from disease. (KR.)

37] THE BOWLES' 50TH WEDDING ANNIVERSARY

Elam Bowles (December 1, 1842–January 1930) was born in Iredell County. As a young man he worked as a farmer in Wilkes County. On April 5, 1862, at the age of 19, he enlisted with Co. F, 52nd NC Infantry, along with his brother Simpson, who was 24. On October 14, 1863, Elam was wounded during the Battle of Bristol Station, Virginia. He was hospitalized at Charlottesville, but returned to duty in less than a month. During the Battle of Sutherland's Station, Virginia, he was captured and confined at Point Lookout until being released on June 23, 1865. To his credit, he participated in the Battles of Goldsboro, Gettysburg, Bristol Station, The Wilderness, Spotsylvania, Petersburg, and Sutherland's Station. In 1866, he married Nancy Matilda Pardue and they had 13 children. Elam spent the last 23 years of his life in Winston-Salem, where he is buried in the Waughtown Cemetery. In this photograph of Elam and Nancy's 50th wedding anniversary are the following, from left to right: (front row) Ida, Elam, Nancy, and Jennie; (back row) Blanche, Robert, Charles, James, Ednte, Bamey, Nora, and Gilmer. (JTM.)

38] JESSE KIMBAROUGH AND JULIA ANN ROBERTS COCKERHAM

Jesse Kimbarough Cockerham poses with his wife, Julia Ann Roberts. Mamie Florence Cockerham Thompson, their daughter, wrote the following passage on February 22, 1999.

> I am ninety-three years old, and to the best of my knowledge at the time of this writing, I am the only living child of a Civil War Veteran in Surry County, NC. My Papa, Jessie Kimbarough Cockerham was born Oct. 9, 1845. When he was fourteen years old, his father, John E. Cockerham and his brother Pleasant Henderson "Bunty" Cockerham, were 'drafted' into the service of the Confederate Army. While they were serving in the Army, the family suffered many hardships. Typhoid Fever swept the area and Papa, his mother Emily, and his sister Sarah all came down with it. Papa survived, but his mother and sister did not. They died in June of 1860. Papa's father, John E. Cockerham, was badly burned while he was serving up in Virginia. The last they heard from him he had taken gangrene and was in a hospital there. He died Dec. 6, 1861 and was buried somewhere in Virginia. Attempts by his children and grandchildren to locate his grave have been unsuccessful. On Mar. 31, 1862, at the young age of sixteen, Papa enlisted with Co. H, 54th Regiment, NC Infantry of the Confederate Army under Captain David S. Cockerham from Jonesville, NC. While serving the Southern Cause, he was shot and wounded while his regiment was retreating across a fence. He got to come home for several weeks while he recuperated before returning to the war. He served three and half years, was twice wounded and finally captured in Petersburg,

37] The Bowles' 50th Wedding Anniversary

38] Jesse Kimbarough and Julia Ann Roberts Cockerham

VA on Apr. 3, 1865. He was then taken to Harts Island, NY where he was confined in a Union Prison until he took the Oath of Allegiance on June 17, 1865. At the end of the war he was released and given a blanket. He walked home (to Surry County, NC). Once he was home he tried to go back to school, but said he could not study for hearing gunshots. Papa was married four times. His first wife was Julia Ann Roberts, who he married on June 10, 1869. They had six children: Susan "Ada," Pinkney Kimber, Sophia Emily, Edwin Thompson, and Julia Ann. Papa said that they grew corn, and raised hogs. He banked $100.00 a year for 13 years. Julia died in childbirth along with her sixth child Oct. 22, 1881. After losing their mother, the small children worked very close with their father. They cooked in iron kettles in the fireplace, and used candles and lanterns for light. They had been taught to make clothes and to knit. They washed their laundry in the creek. Papa married his second wife Elizabeth "Bettie" Moody on Aug. 11, 1883. Elizabeth and her infant son died Sept. 17, 1884. He married his third wife, Melvina "Mel" Jones, on Feb. 6, 1886. Mel died July 4, 1904. They had no children. Papa's fourth marriage was to my mother, Mary Elizabeth "Ida" White Snow. They were married Feb. 12, 1905. Papa was fifty-nine years old and Mama was thirty-four. Mama was a widow with one son Cleat Snow by her first husband William "Dobb" Snow. My twin brother James Elmer and myself were born Feb. 22, 1906. My younger sister and Papa's youngest child, Corabetti Pearl, was born Mar. 9, 1908. Papa was 62 years old. People told him he would never live to see us raised. He proved them wrong. Papa died at the age of 86 on Mar. 20, 1932. Elmer and I were twenty-six years old and Pearl was twenty-four. When I was young we lived in a two story house. One day when I was eleven years old, we went to visit a sick neighbor, Joshua Adams, and while we were gone the house caught fire and burned to the ground. We had a large one room granary that we had to move in. Papa built a fireplace in it. There was a shed on the side of the granary that Papa kept his buggy in, he closed that in to make another room. We lived there for four years until the new house was built. He built us an "L" shaped log house. It had three rooms downstairs with a double fireplace. One fireplace was in the kitchen so we could stay warm and cook on the fireplace hearth. It also had two bedrooms and a loft upstairs. We raised geese for the down for feather beds and pillows. When Papa was seventy-one years old, he talked about being old, but he worked hard. My brother Elmer and I helped him to cut logs off the farm to build a new house. The neighbors came and had a barn raising. They put the logs up in two days. Old man Case Bryant came and stood on the scaffold and hewed the logs after they were put up. Mama, me, and a friend Ethel Hanes, cooked dinner. We made corn bread in a skillet in the fireplace and pies and sweet potatoes. Papa loved his family and his community. A sip of homemade whiskey for every member of the family each morning was a rule for good health. A special day was set aside for corn-shucking. Neighbors would come to help shuck the corn and enjoy the food, music and dancing. (JC and AS.)

39] SAMUEL LAWRENCE HAUER

Samuel Lawrence Hauser (December 13, 1835–September 25, 1924) was born in Stokes County to Samuel Thomas and Anna Maria Hege Hauser. He married Sybilla Louisa Hauser on November 21, 1857, and the two had eight children. On March 26, 1862, at the age of 26, he enlisted in the Co. D, 53rd NC Infantry, Daniel's Brigade. This regiment "received its first baptism of fire" in Washington, North Carolina. As an integral part of the Army of Northern

39] SAMUEL LAWRENCE HAUER

Virginia, it participated in more than 20 general engagements, marching and fighting from Fredericksburg to Appomattox. On September 22, 1864, during the Battle of Fisher's Hill, Samuel was captured and imprisoned at Point Lookout. He remained there until his parole on March 17, 1865. He was received at Boulware's Wharf, James River, Virginia, on March 19, 1865, for exchange. He died on September 25, 1924, in the county where he was born. (SC.)

40] ALEXANDER MARTIN "SQUIRE ECK" BOYLES

Alexander Martin "Squire Eck" Boyles (August 2, 1844–December 25, 1929) was born in Stokes County to Solomon and Elizabeth Boles Boyles. He was a farmer all his life, and was called "Squire Eck" by others to distinguish him from the other two men with the same name in his community. He volunteered with Co. H, 53rd NC Infantry, the Danbury Blues, on March 20, 1862, at the age of 17. The 53rd traveled to New Bern, entering into its first engagement at Washington, North Carolina, in the winter of 1862. A few days after the Battle of Chancellorsville, the 53rd became part of the Army of Northern Virginia. Attached to Daniel's Brigade, he marched and fought from Fredericksburg to Appomattox, participating in more than 20 general engagements. On July 6, 1864, Alexander was promoted to first sergeant and listed present or accounted for through August 1864. On September 22, 1864, during the Battle of Fisher Hill, he was injured and hospitalized. While recovering in the Richmond hospital, he was taken prisoner, and was confined to Point Lookout on October 18, 1864. He eventually received a parole and was transferred to Venus Point, Savannah River, Georgia, for exchange. By February 1865, Alexander again reported for duty. During the Battle of Fort

71

40] ALEXANDER MARTIN
"SQUIRE ECK" BOYLES

41] ALEXANDER WILLIAM WESTMORELAND

42] JOSEPH H. STEWART AND
ALFRED SHELTON STEWART

43] JOHN WESLEY ARMSWORTH

Stedman on March 25, 1865, he was injured and hospitalized in Richmond. The hospital fell once more into Union hands, and on April 3, 1865, he was again taken prisoner and confined to Point Lookout, where he remained imprisoned until being released on June 26, 1865, after signing the Oath of Allegiance. He returned to farming, but also served as a justice of the peace in Stokes County. He was well known for recalling the stories of his years of service in the Civil War. On September 8, 1868, he married Mary Frances Page, and the two had the following children: Nannie Lee, Ernest, Walter, James, Rosey Ellen, Gaston, Lillian Alice, Carrie Frances, Daisy Belle, and Reid. Alexander died in Yadkin Township, Stokes County. (SCT.)

41] ALEXANDER WILLIAM WESTMORELAND

Alexander William Westmoreland (July 29, 1835–April 20, 1923), the son of William W. and Charity Morris Westmoreland, was born in Stokes County, in the Little Yadkin area. On May 20, 1854, he married Elizabeth Matilda "Bettie" Dean (September 9, 1836–January 10, 1899), the daughter of Abner Harrison and Susannah "Sucky" Johnson Dean. Elizabeth was born and died in Carroll County, Virginia. She and Alexander had ten children. At the time of his enlistment on May 17, 1862, Alexander was working as a cabinetmaker. He mustered in as sergeant with Co. D, 53rd NC Infantry, and was promoted to first sergeant prior to September 1, 1862. He was reported present on surviving company muster rolls through February 1863. Elected second lieutenant on June 27, 1863, he was listed present or accounted for through August 1864. During the Battle of Winchester on September 19, 1864, he sustained wounds in the calf of his right leg. He was captured and hospitalized in the Union hospital in Baltimore. On December 9, 1864, he was transferred to Fort McHenry, and on January 1, 1865, he was moved to Fort Delaware. That following June, he was released after taking the Oath of Allegiance. Long after the war, on August 27, 1900, Alexander married a second time, to Laura A. Combs. Less than three years later, on August 1, 1903, he married for a third time, to Mary Virginia Tate. He applied for a pension for his military service on August 31, 1909; in his application he stated that he was 74 years old and that, for the past 39 years, had lived in Virginia working as a millwright. On May 21, 1910, he received an annual pension of $36. He is buried in the Tolbert-Westmoreland Cemetery in Carroll County. (JSB.)

42] JOSEPH H. STEWART AND ALFRED SHELTON STEWART

Joseph H. Stewart (left) and Alfred Shelton Stewart pose for a photograph. Joseph was born on April 20, 1845, in Stokes County. On March 20, 1862, at the age of 18, he enlisted with Co. H, 53rd Regiment, NC Troops. During the Battle of Gettysburg, he sustained wounds in the right shoulder and left hand (the latter required the amputation of two fingers) before being taken prisoner. He was paroled shortly thereafter, on July 30, 1863, and was received at City Point on August 1, 1863, for exchange. He returned for duty in January 1864. On October 25, 1864, he was captured again, this time at Cedar Creek, Virginia, and he was confined at Point Lookout until June 19, 1865, when he took the Oath of Allegiance. Alfred S. Stewart (August 13, 1836–March 9, 1920) enlisted on October 14, 1862, at the age of 26 with Co. H, 53rd NC Infantry. Surviving company muster rolls show he was present or accounted for through October 1863. He then reported for duty as a provost guard at corp headquarters, where he served from November 1863 through February 1865. (BL.)

43] JOHN WESLEY ARMSWORTH

John Wesley Armsworth enlisted on April 17, 1862, at the age of 32. Up until the time of his enlistment with Co. H, 54th NC Infantry, he farmed in Yadkin County. He was reported as AWOL in June 1862, but returned to duty prior to January 1, 1863. John was captured near Fredericksburg on May 4, 1863. After his confinement at the Old Capitol Prison in Washington, D.C., he was paroled and exchanged on May 23, 1863, at City Point. He returned to duty and was promoted to sergeant on September 1, 1863. Two months later, during the battle at Rappahannock Station, Virginia, he was wounded in the right arm and captured. He was again sent to Washington, D.C., where he was hospitalized. He died about February 1, 1864, of "pyemia." (NCA.)

44] JOSEPH SINCLAIR AND EMILY JANE IDOL RAGSDALE JR.

Joseph Sinclair Ragsdale Jr. (November 11, 1836–May 5, 1903) was born in Greensboro, Guilford County. Prior to the war, he earned his living as a schoolteacher. He enlisted on May 27, 1862, with Co. F, 54th NC Infantry, mustering in as first sergeant. He was promoted to second lieutenant on September 13, 1862. That following November, he began suffering from an abscess in his upper jaw and he entered General Hospital No. 8 (St. Charles Hospital) in Richmond. He received a sick furlough for 40 days. He then returned to duty and was present or accounted for through December 1863. During the Battle of Drewry's Bluff, Virginia, in May of 1864, he was wounded in the thigh and confined to the Chimborazo Hospital No. 4, Richmond. He returned to duty on September 22, 1864, after another 40-day furlough. During the Battle of Fisher's Hill, he was captured and confined to Fort Delaware. He was released on June 8, 1865, after taking the Oath of Allegiance. After the war, Joseph returned to his home and courted Miss Emily Jane Idol (February 25, 1841–June 24, 1934). When the time came to propose marriage, Joseph wrote to Jane of his affection:

> I have marched the winter's snow about frozen to death and in the summer heat nearly dying of thirst. My clothes have been pierced by the balls of the enemy. My sword case has been shot in two at my side. I have faced death on fifty battlefields. I have lain wounded amid the thunder of artillery and the fellow mortals dying at my side, thinking that my life's blood was fast flowing out. In all these things my heart was unconquered. But now that heart gives up itself and asks only to be the captive of you its captor. I now come to you and ask your hand in marriage. I have only an humble, faithful affectionate heart to offer you—the heart of a temperate man—a temperance amounting to a total abstinence from all that intoxicates. I can promise no palatial home, no road of ease and luxury. I am poor—but thank heavens I believe that I have the energy to make a living. I refer you to the company in which I served for my character during the war. I joined it as a private unknown to all except a few. I may say in self-defense that I was promoted four times by the acclamation of the officers and men of the company, and recommended and commissioned without examination . . .

The two were married in Friendship, Guilford County, on June 10, 1866. Joseph died in Charlotte on May 5, 1903, and Emily died in Jamestown on June 24, 1934. In 1991, their home, Magnolia Farm, was placed on the National Register of Historic Places. (FH.)

44] Joseph Sinclair and Emily Jane Idol Ragsdale Jr.

45] William Alfred Caudle

46] Augustus C. Vogler

45] WILLIAM ALFRED CAUDLE

William Alfred Caudle was born about 1838 to Richard and Rebecca Childress Caudle of Halifax County. He enlisted as a private on July 11, 1861, at the age of 22 for a period of 12 months. He was attached to Co. E., 59th Regiment, VA Infantry, the Bruce Guards. William was captured by the Federal invasion force commanded by Gen. Ambrose E. Burnside at the Battle of Roanoke Island on February 8, 1862. General Burnside paroled the captured Confederates at Elizabeth City, North Carolina, because he did not want to spare his troops to guard them. Burnside's men noted that the Tar Heels accepted their paroles without comment, but the Virginians were belligerent even though they were prisoners. William rejoined the regiment later in the year and received a promotion to third corporal. The unit was involved in the Peninsula Campaign of Virginia; the defense of Charleston in 1863; the defense of northeast Florida in early 1864; and the siege of Petersburg in 1864–65. His brothers, James Washington and Robert B. Caudle, were also in the 59th. William and James survived the war, but Robert died of disease in 1864. On March 12, 1867, William married Permelia Pulliam, the daughter of Drewry and Eliza Griffin Pulliam, in Halifax County. The couple moved to Stokes County in 1875, no doubt to join his brother James, who was living in Stokes County at that time. Though William was not connected to any North Carolina regiment, many of his descendants presently live in Stokes County, and requested his photograph be included. (SC.)

46] AUGUSTUS C. VOGLER

Augustus C. Vogler (January 15, 1831–March 22, 1865) was born in Salem to Peter and Sarah (Sally) Vogler. On December 22, 1857, he married Elisa Epsey Blackburn, and the couple had three children: Sarah J., Lewis Monroe, and William Francis Vogler. Augustus joined Co. D, 57th NC Infantry, enlisting as a private for three years of service or the duration of the war. From Winston, he traveled with his regiment to Salisbury, where he officially mustered in on July 17, 1862. He then traveled to Richmond and was attached to Davis' Brigade, General W. Smith's Division. He suffered from "debilitas," resulting in his hospitalization in Richmond on September 22, 1862. Two months later he was admitted to Moore Hospital in Richmond with typhoid fever. He returned home to Winston to convalesce until his sick leave furlough ran out in December 1862. By May 1863, the 57th Regiment was at Marye's Heights, near Fredericksburg, eventually arriving in Gettysburg on July 2, 1863. Augustus was captured the next day. He was confined at Fort McHenry, Maryland, then transferred to Fort Delaware. On October 22, 1863, he was transferred to Point Lookout, where he died on March 22, 1865, from "chronic diarrhoea." He is interred in Grave No. 1372 in the Prisoner of War Graveyard at Point Lookout. On June 26, 1890, Epsey applied for the Act for Relief of Widows. (FJM.)

47] MEMBERS OF THE 58TH REGIMENT

In late 1861, John B. Palmer recruited a legion of cavalry, infantry, and artillery from the North Carolina mountains near Mitchell County. Most of these men worked small farms, had few (if any) slaves, and they had little interest in the war at all, but rather than being conscripted into a Southern regiment, they enlisted voluntarily. The three cavalry companies

47] MEMBERS OF THE 58TH REGIMENT

48] GEORGE WASHINGTON FINLEY
HARPER AND JAMES C. HARPER

49] PHILIP ALEXANDER HAUSER

became the core of the 5th NC Cavalry Battalion, which was later consolidated with the 7th NC Cavalry Battalion to form the 65th NC State Troops or 6th NC Cavalry. The 58th NC was originally known as the 58th NC Partisan Rangers, and was later redesignated the 58th NC State Troops. The soldiers in the photograph to the left are as follows: (bottom) Pvt. J.L. Craig; (lower left) Sgt. E.L. Moore; (lower right) Sgt. A.C. Craig; (middle) Lt. Col. Edmund Kirby; (top) Lt. Col. S.M. Silver; (top left) Capt. L.W. Gilbert; (top right) Sgt. E.H. Crump. In the photograph to the right they are as follows: (bottom) Sgt.-Maj. Drury D. Coffey; (lower left) Capt. Isaac H. Bailey; (lower right) Capt. F.A. Tobey; (top) Col. John B. Palmer; (top left) Capt. Benjamin F. Baird; (top right) Maj. G.W.F. Harper. (NCR.)

48] GEORGE WASHINGTON FINLEY HARPER

George Washington Finley Harper was born at Fairfield to James and Caroline Ellen Finley Harper (the daughter of Samuel Finley of Londonderry, Ireland). George enlisted as a private with Co. H., 58th Regiment, NC Infantry, Partisan's Rangers, organized in Mitchell County. This regiment became a part of three arms of service commanded by Col. John B. Palmer. By 1864, George had reached the rank of major. He was present, with his regiment, during the surrender at Greensboro, North Carolina, in April 1865. After the war, he went into business with his father. J. Harper & Son became well known and successful merchants in and around their community. In 1881, George was elected a member of the NC State Legislature, and he served on many boards of benevolent institutions. He established the Bank of Lenoir, and was one of the builders of the Carolina & Northwestern Railroad, serving as the president of both. In 1910, in association with Judge Walter Clark, he published *Caldwell County in the Great War*. For that work, he wrote the chapters "North Carolina at Chickamauga," "A War Time Furlough," "Kirk's Raid and Skirmish," and "Sherman in Columbia." In addition to these articles, George compiled and published a valuable local history book entitled *Reminiscences of Caldwell County in the Great War*. He is shown here with one of his grandsons, James C. Harper.

49] PHILIP ALEXANDER HAUSER

Philip Alexander Hauser (1843–1929) enlisted with Co. G, 57th NC Regiment, on March 9, 1862. He was captured near Petersburg, Virginia, on October 27, 1864. Judging by the pin on his lapel, he was attending a Confederate veteran's reunion at the time this photograph was taken. (NCR.)

Five

TWENTY-SIXTH REGIMENT:
A HOME FOR SALEM'S BAND

THE 26TH REGIMENTAL BAND poses while on furlough, July-August 1862, at their hometown of Salem, North Carolina. From left to right are James M. Fisher, Julius A. Leinbach, Daniel T. Crouse, Augustus L. Hauser, William H. Hall, Joe O. Hall, Abe P. Gibson, and Capt. Samuel T. Mickey. The 26th Regimental Band was regarded as one of the best in the Army of Northern Virginia. The original band members were citizens of the township of Salem, as well as members of the Moravian Church. In addition to their musical responsibilities, these men also assisted medical and ambulance personnel. In some cases they were responsible for the burying of amputated limbs. When the soldiers became exhausted, Mickey's musicians would gather their instruments and strike up inspirational tunes to boost the morale of their comrades. Occasionally, during these impromptu concerts, the rumble of artillery would almost cease, as the soldiers of both sides listened proudly to their regimental bands compete with each other across the battlefield. (MMF.)

1] AUGUSTUS LEWIS
"GUS" HAUSER

2] DANIEL T.
CROUSE

3] JOSEPH O.
HALL

4] JAMES M. FISHER

5] SARAH MALINDA
PRITCHARD "SAM" BLALOCK

6] WILLIAM A. LEMLY

1] AUGUSTUS LEWIS "GUS" HAUSER

Augustus Lewis "Gus" Hauser (March 25, 1841–November 23, 1862) was born in Salem. Like the other members of the 26th Regimental Band, Gus was a Moravian. The Moravian religion objected to participation in the war, but considered serving as a musician acceptable. At the age of only 21, Gus became ill and died while home on furlough. From his death came the fifth recruit of the band, Henry A. Siddall. On November 30, 1862, while on his way to join the 55th Regiment, Henry was approached by a neighbor, Sam Leinback, who asked him to join the 26th Regimental Band instead. Eager to serve in a regiment of familiar faces, Henry decided to join the band as their second E flat coronetist. (SC.)

2] DANIEL T. CROUSE

Daniel T. Crouse (May 19, 1836–1903) enlisted in Craven County on May 24, 1861, to serve as a private with Co. E, 26th NC Infantry. On July 14, 1861, he transferred to the 26th Regimental Band after his promotion to musician. On April 1, 1865, Daniel was captured at Amelia Court House, Virginia and he was imprisoned at Point Lookout until June 1865. After the war, he became well known for his excellence in teaching and encouraging young Salem boys to play brass instruments. One of his students was Mr. B.J. Pfohl, who conducted the Salem band for over 50 years. (MMF.)

3] JOSEPH O. HALL

Joseph O. Hall (March 29, 1834–June 30, 1890) was born to James and Sarah Hall. The 1850 Forsyth County census lists him with his siblings, his father, James, and his mother, Sarah H. Joseph married his first wife, Louisa Sophia Smith, on October 7, 1857. During the war he served with the 26th Regimental Band with his brother, William H. Hall. Sadly, while the band was on furlough in Salem, Joseph's nephew Gussie died. Joseph and his fellow band members played at the funeral. After the war, he settled once more in his hometown of Salem, and began a confection and baking business with his brother William at the corner of South Main and Academy Street. In 1869, at the age of 34, Louisa died in Winston of typhoid fever, leaving Joseph to care for their two small children. After his second marriage, he no longer attended the Moravian church, choosing instead to worship in the Presbyterian church. He is buried in the Presbyterian section of Salem Cemetery. (MMF.)

4] JAMES M. FISHER

James M. Fisher was an active member of the Moravian Salem Band before the war, but he was not one of the original members of the 26th Regimental Band. For this photograph, he borrowed the uniform of Alexander C. Meining, who had taken ill and could not be present. After the war, James continued his trade in Winston Township as a baker and confectionist. His wife was Frances L. Benzien; the two were married on July 8, 1854. Their son, Charles L., worked as a clerk in a dry goods store. Daughters Emma and Elfleda attended school. The baby of the household, Louisa, was only three years old at the time of this photograph. In February of 1874, at the age of 56, James died at his residence in Salem after a lingering illness. He was buried with Masonic honors. (MMF.)

5] SARAH MALINDA PRITCHARD "SAM" BLALOCK

Sarah Malinda Pritchard "Sam" Blalock was born in Alexander County. She married William McKesson "Keith" Blalock in 1856. When North Carolina seceded, the Blalocks, who were pro-Unionists, were living in Watauga County, near Grandfather Mountain. Sarah knew Keith would eventually be drafted into the Confederacy, so they set in motion a plan for his enlistment and desertion. She, however, had no intention of being left behind. She cut off her hair, found suitable clothing, adopted the name "Sam," and on March 20, 1862, she and her husband enlisted in Co. F, 26th NC Infantry, the Hibriten Guards. She is one of only two women known to have served in any NC Confederate regiment. Records described "Sam" as "a good looking boy . . . weight about 130 pounds, five feet, four inches." It was amazing that her real identity was never revealed. She marched and drilled like any other member of the company. She tented with her husband, and was very adept at learning camp life. The couple's plan for an early desertion was thwarted many times. They simply could not reach the Union line. Desperate to get out of the army, Keith covered himself with poison sumac, creating a severe allergic reaction with "many loathsome skin eruptions." The surgeons agreed that he was unfit for service and discharged him on April 20, 1862, citing "hernia" and "poison from sumac." Sarah immediately revealed her disguise and was promptly discharged along with her husband. (CVM.)

6] WILLIAM A. LEMLY

William A. Lemly (c. 1846–1928) was born in Bethania to Henry A. and Amanda Conrad Lemly. He received his education at the Boys' School in Salem, North Carolina. At the age of 17, he gave up his studies and entered the Confederate Army, serving as a musician in the 26th Regimental Band until his capture near Petersburg in April 1865. He was interred at Point Lookout until his release the following June. During the earliest days of reconstruction, Israel G. Lash, William's uncle, founded the First National Bank of Salem. Years later, when Israel died, the bank was reorganized and became the Wachovia Bank. William originally served as the bank's cashier, but eventually became its president. In 1874 he married Salem-native Bertha C. Belo, the daughter of Edward and Carolina Amanda (Fries) Belo and the sister of Col. Alfred Belo. When Bertha died in 1883, William married again, this time to Emily Louisa de Schweinitz, the daughter of Emil Adolphus and Sophia Amelia (Hermann) de Schweinitz of Salem. He died in Winston-Salem, Forsyth County.

7] SAMUEL TIMOTHY MICKEY   8] ALEXANDER MEINUNG

7] SAMUEL TIMOTHY MICKEY

Samuel Timothy Mickey was about 30 years old at the time of his enlistment. Many of his neighbors and relatives were members of the 11th and 33rd NC Regimental Bands, and had left for the war already. Samuel, anxious to find a regimental assignment for his newly assembled band, traveled to New Bern and approached Col. Zeb Vance for an assignment. Familiar with the excellence of the Salem Band, Colonel Vance quickly agreed, assigning Samuel and his band to the 26th Regiment, NC Troops. The band reported at Camp French on November 1, 1862, and assumed their duties of playing every morning for guard mount, every evening at dress parade, and giving a short concert every night. During the battle at the Amelia Court House in April 1865, Mickey and other members of his band were captured and confined to Point Lookout. He was released June 29, 1865, after taking the Oath of Allegiance. On November 10, 1870, Samuel married Pauline Susan Hege (January 2, 1840–December 15, 1912), the daughter of Christian and Anna M. Hege. The couple had four children: Carrie Anna, Minnie Salome, Edward Timothy, and Robert Hege Mickey. (MMF.)

8] ALEXANDER MEINUNG

Alexander Meinung (April 25, 1823–April 15, 1908) was one of the original members of the 26th Regimental Band. Aside from his musical talents, he was also an accomplished sketch artist. His collection of about 80 wartime sketches were intact until about 1985, when a dealer broke up the collection through various sales. Many of his original sketches are in the Southern Historical Collection at Chapel Hill, along with Julius Leinbach's original diary. Alexander was

9] Members of the 26th Regiment

apparently unhappy with his lot as a musician. His compiled service record reveals three separate attempts to secure a transfer to the CS Topographical Engineer Department as a cartographer. All three requests were denied. After the war, he became a professor at Salem Academy, where he taught organ, piano, and clarinet. He conducted the Salem Orchestra and played the organ at the Home Moravian Church. He died in Winston-Salem and is buried in the Moravian Cemetery. (COS.)

9] MEMBERS OF THE 26TH REGIMENT

The 26th Regiment fought in some of the bloodiest battles recorded in American history. Eighteen-year-old Col. Harry K. Burgwyn, a graduate of the U.S. Military Academy and the Virginia Military Institute, was one of the youngest regimental commanders in the Confederate Army. He held the rank of major at the start of the war; upon the organization of the 26th Regiment at Camp Carolina in 1861, he was promoted to the rank of lieutenant colonel, and when Colonel Vance was elected as governor of North Carolina in 1862, he was promoted to colonel, assuming command of the 26th Regiment, NC Troops. On July 1, 1863, the first day of the Battle of Gettysburg, the 26th fought fiercely, breaking through the Federal line and forcing the Yankees to withdraw from the field. The goal of this battle was achieved, but at a great loss to the regiment. Out of 800 men taken into the fight that morning, 588 were killed, wounded, or missing, and the regimental colors were shot down 14 times. On July 3, 1863, the 26th Regiment continued the Gettysburg Campaign with the Pettigrew-Trimble-Pickett Assault. Their regimental colors were shot down 8 more times. Over 120 more men were lost or killed, including Colonel Burgwyn. Co. F, the Hibriten Guards, suffered a 100 percent loss. The regimental losses of the 26th at Gettysburg were the "greatest in percent and the greatest in number sustained in any one battle, of any of the 2,500 regiments which both sides sent into that great struggle." After Gettysburg the 26th continued its service under A.P. Hill. It went on to fight in The Wilderness and the defense of Petersburg. Throughout the war the 26th continued to support other Confederate forces against the Union, earning their nickname: "The Bloody 26th." They surrendered with General Lee at Appomattox Court House. The members of the 26th Regiment in the images on the opposite page are as follows: *upper left image:* (lower left) Capt. and Asst. Quarter Master J.J. Young; (lower, middle) Col. Harry Burgwyn; (lower right) Adj. James B. Gordon; (middle, left) Maj. N.P. Rankin; (middle, right) Surgeon Thomas J. Boykin; (top left) Col. John R. Lane; (top, middle) Col. Zebulon B. Vance; and (top right) Lt. Col. John T. Jones; *upper right image, clockwise from top*: Capt. Samuel P. Wagg, Co. A; Capt. Stephen W. Brewer, Co. E.; Capt. R.M. Tuttle, Co. F; Capt. H.C. Albright, Co. G; Capt. Joseph R. Ballew, Co. F; Capt. William Wilson, Co. B; and (center) Lt. Col. James T. Adams; *lower left image, clockwise from top*: unidentifed; Pvt. W.W. Edwards, Co. E; Pvt. H.C. Coffey, Co. F; Pvt. Laban Ellis, Co. E; Pvt. J.D. Moore, Co. F; Sec. Lt. Wm. N. Snelling, Co. F; and (center) Sgt. John Tuttle, Co. F; *lower right image, clockwise from top*: Asst. Surg. W.W. Gaither; Capt. James McLaughlen; Frst. Lt. Orran Hanner; Frst. Lt. J.G. Jones; Frst. Lt. George Wilcox; Capt. Thomas Lilly; and (center) Capt. J.D. McIver. (NCR.)

10] JULIUS ABRAHAM TRANSOU

Julius Abraham Transou (January 1, 1832–January 21, 1930) was born to Philip and Mary Stoltz Transou. Prior to his enlistment, he worked with his father and brothers in the wagonmaking trade. He married Julia Sybilla Conrad on June 10, 1855, and built a seven-room log house for his growing family of six children. Desiring to join the 26th Regimental Band, Julius enlisted in March 1862 and reported for duty in Kinston, where the regiment was camped. He was no stranger to the other band members, as he was a fellow Moravian from the township of Bethania, located near Salem. He served as the band's first cornetist and later, solo Eb alto. During the bloody battles of April 1865, Julius was captured at Petersburg and sent to Point Lookout. Like many of his comrades, he returned home extremely ill. He made a living as a piano tuner traveling around North Carolina, and was also the local cobbler in his village of Bethania. At age 90, he began making his funeral arrangements complete with a horse-drawn wagon, the music to be played (some of which he had composed), the logistics of the service and interment, who would sit where, and so on. At the age of 95, the newspaper from a nearby city sent a reporter to interview the old gentleman and write a story about his Civil War experiences and to what he attributed his longevity. When the story was published in the newspaper, the "old man" blew a gasket and ranted for several hours about how he had become a "damned curiosity" and didn't understand why he couldn't just die and go on. He had not realized his visitor was from the newspaper, but instead thought the reporter was a passerby stopping to rest and talk for a while, which was a rather common occurrence. Upon Julius's death on January 21, 1930, his funeral arrangements were carried out to the letter—even to his daughter and her daughter-in-law singing a hymn he had composed in the 1860s while serving in the regimental band serving as one of "Lee's Miserables." (MATNF.)

11] William Henry Hall

William Henry Hall (October 25, 1829–September 20, 1897) was born in Salem. On August 16, 1854, he married Ernestine "Stiney" Augusta Vierling (September 26, 1833–January 22, 1893), who was also born in Salem. William had a reputation as an expert beekeeper and studied the confectionery business in Philadelphia. He was known as the "candy maker" of Salem. At his enlistment with the 26th Regimental Band, he left his wife and four small children and traveled to New Bern, North Carolina, with his fellow band members. In 1862, during the month of July, he accompanied his fellow band members back to Salem on a much-needed furlough. They anticipated performing many concerts for their community. Sadly, their first musical performance was for the funeral of Gussie, one of William's children. As condolences to the family were made, the band rendered appropriate chorales at the internment. What was to have been a happy homecoming for the Hall family, became instead a period of mourning. In 1863, during the confusion of the retreat from Gettysburg, William found himself separated from his fellow band members. He was captured in Greencastle during an attack on a Confederate wagon train, and was imprisoned at Point Lookout, Maryland, where he remained until the end of the war. In November of 1863, Edward A. Brietz, a fellow "Salemite," took his place in the band. Shortly thereafter, Edward was promoted to lieutenant of the 26th NC Regiment and was transferred out of the band. (MMF.)

12] A "Programme" for a Show by "Guss Rich"

William Augustus Reich (or "Guss Rich," as he came to be known) was born on July 16, 1833, in Forsyth County. His parents, Jacob and Ann Reich, owned a coppersmith shop on the corner of Blum and Main Streets. Gus worked there as a tinner. Aside from his "day job,"

10] JULIUS ABRAHAM TRANSOU

11] WILLIAM HENRY HALL

12] A "PROGRAMME"
FOR A SHOW BY "GUSS RICH"

13] JULIUS
AUGUSTUS LINEBACH

he was also a magician, and he became famous as the "The Wizard of the Blue Ridge." His first public performance was in 1860, in the Salem Concert Hall. During the war he served as a drummer for the 26th Regimental Band under the leadership of Samuel Mickey. The band received several short furloughs over the course of the war to perform concerts at nearby cities. Not only were the band members known far and wide for their musical talents, but the "Wizard's" magic show was not to be missed! From these concerts, thousands of dollars were raised for the Confederate cause. After procuring their much needed supplies, they would donate money to the local relief societies and hospitals. After returning from the war, Gus married Miss Mary Kitchell. From 1871 to 1873, they lived in Mt. Airy, where he opened a tinshop. During this period he was consigned to build a special oversized coffin for his neighbors, the famous Siamese twins, Eng and Chang Bunker. (SHC.)

13] Julius Augustus Linebach

Julius Augustus Linebach (September 8, 1834–February 21, 1930) was one of the eight original bandsmen of the 26th Regimental Band. He kept an in-depth diary of his experiences during his service. During their campaigns, one of the other band members, Alex Meinung, would occasionally sketch their encampments to accompany Julius's entries. Julius was the last of the band to be released when he was paroled on June 28, 1865. He reached High Point by train and then walked home, arriving soon after noon on Sunday, July 2, 1865. Following the war, he engaged in several business enterprises. His most rewarding responsibility was that of secretary-treasurer of the Moravian Church, Southern Province, a position his brother had held for many years. His original diary and some of the sketchings are archived in the Southern Historical Collection, Chapel Hill. (MMF.)

Six

TWENTY-FIRST REGIMENT:
REMEMBERING OUR MEN

UNIDENTIFIED OFFICERS OF CO. D, 21ST REGIMENT, NC INFANTRY, pose for a photographer. When North Carolina seceded in May of 1861, the state government called for volunteers and enlisted men to serve the Confederacy. During the months of May and June, 12 companies of infantry were organized as the 11th Infantry Regiment, NC Volunteers. The following November, this regiment was redesignated as the 21st Regiment, NC Infantry. The regiment served throughout the entire war, and was present at the surrender at Appomattox. The companies were organized as follows: Co. A, the Davidson Guards of Davidson County; Co. B, the Yadkin Gray Eagles of Yadkin County; Co. C, Blue Ridge Riflemen of Surry County; Co. D, Forsyth Rifles of Forsyth County; Co. E, Forsyth Grays and Forsyth Guards from Forsyth County; Co. F, the Mountain Boys of Stokes County; Co. G, the Town Fork Invincibles of Stokes County; Co. H, the Mountain Tigers of Surry County; Co. I, the Surry Marksmen of Surry County; Co. K, the Forsyth Southrons of Forsyth County; Co. L, the Rockingham Invincibles of Rockingham County; and Co. M, the Guilford Dixie Boys of Guilford County. (NCR.)

1] THE 11TH REGIMENT, NC VOLUNTEERS

2] JAMES FRANKLIN BEALL

3] BENNETT AND WILLIAM ELIAS SPACH

1] THE 11TH REGIMENT, NC VOLUNTEERS

The 11th Regiment, NC Volunteers are shown here in Danville, Virginia, in June 1861. The Forsyth Rifles (Co. D), commanded by Capt. Alfred H. Belo, was organized in Salem on May 21, 1861, making it the first company organized in Forsyth County. The Forsyth Grays (Co. E.), commanded by Capt. Rufus W. Wharton, was organized in Salem three days later. The Forsyth Southrons (Co. K), commanded by Capt. F.P. Miller, was organized in Winston on June 11, 1861. Before the troops departed, the young ladies of Salem presented to Captain Belo the flag of the Forsyth Rifles, which they had tirelessly sewn from red, white, and blue silk. The flag contained a circle of 15 six-pointed stars, and embroidered upon the bars are the motto "Liberty or Death" and the legend "Forsyth Rifles No Ca." (It is presently on display at the Museum of the Confederacy in Richmond, Virginia.) In Belo's, memoirs he described, "The leave-taking was very pathetic. We marched down past the Moravian Girl's School, where, with all the people standing by to bid us Godspeed, Bishop Bahnson of the Moravian Church gave us his blessing." The regiment marched to the edge of town, where they boarded their wagons for the journey to Danville. They eventually arrived at Camp Hill, joining the other companies from Guilford, Davidson, Yadkin, Surry, Stokes, and Rockingham. These companies were first recognized as the 11th NC Volunteers; they were later redesignated as the 21st NC Troops. (NCR.)

2] JAMES FRANKLIN BEALL

James Franklin Beall was born on September 1, 1837, in Boone Township, the son of Dr. Burgess Lamar Beall and the brother of Capt. Thomas B. Beall of Co. I, 14th NC Regiment. He received his education at the University of North Carolina and the University of Virginia, where he studied medicine with his brother Robert. In June 1861, he volunteered with the 21st Regiment, NC Infantry, and was commissioned to the rank of major. He participated in many of the major battles and was five times wounded. At the close of war, he continued his education at Jefferson Medical College in Philadelphia. Upon graduation, he opened a practice in Cotton Grove Township, where he remained for about 10 years. He was an active member of the Davidson County Medical Society, the NC State Medical Society, and the Lexington Camp of Confederate Veterans. In 1869 he married Cornelia Harper, the daughter of James and Caroline Finley Harper, and the sister of Maj. George W.F. Harper of the 58th NC Infantry. The couple had three children: Carrie, James, and Frank Harper Beall. In 1901, James wrote many compelling accounts of the battles fought by the 21st Regiment. One such account described his brother's fall in the Battle of Fisher's Hill, Virginia:

> During this battle, occurred one of the most trying ordeals of the writer's life. We were moving on the enemy, when the writer met his brother, Capt. T.B. Beall, of the 14th N.C. Regiment, coming out desperately wounded through the lung, the blood spurting from his breast. There wasn't time to give him a word of sympathy, much less attention, leaving him as I then thought for the last time in this world. He had the good fortune soon after, to meet with an ambulance, which took him and the gallant Lieutenant W.G. Foy, of the 21st NC Regiment, who was also desperately wounded, to the field hospital. They received immediate attention, and both finally recovered, but were left more or less disabled for life. In this same battle fell the lamented Ramseur.

3] BENNETT AND WILLIAM ELIAS SPACH

In November 1864, Brothers Bennett (left) and William Elias Spach (right) enlisted in their hometown of Salem with Co. B, 1st Battalion, NC Sharpshooters. Like other young Southern men at the time, they probably believed the war would be more exciting than their present occupation (they were wainwrights). In December 1864, in the dead of winter, their regiment traveled through the Shenandoah Valley, then on to Petersburg. On February 6, 1865, during the Battle of Hatcher's Run, the brothers were captured and placed in Old Capitol Prison. Three weeks later, just three short months after enlisting, they deserted the Confederate Army and signed the Oath of Allegiance. They were released from prison and provided transportation to the Moravian community of Hope, Indiana, where they lived until the end of the war. William returned to building carriages in Salem and married four times, fathering 19 children. Upon his death on February 21, 1891, his obituary described him as "age sixty-two and a well-known and respected citizen of Waughtown." He is buried in the Waughtown Cemetery in Winston-Salem. Bennett briefly operated a sawmill in Lewisville Township, Forsyth County. The 1870 Forsyth County Census lists him as being a 38-year-old farmer living in Broadbay Township with his 26-year-old wife, Caroline, and their three children: Lewis, Sarah, and Charles C. (JTS.)

4] HENRY THEODORE BAHNSON

Henry Theodore Bahnson (March 6, 1845–January 16, 1917) was born in Lancaster, Pennsylvania, the son of Bishop George Frederick and Anna Gertrude Pauline Conrad Bahnson. On January 14, 1863, barely 18 years old, Henry volunteered for Co. B., 1st NC Battalion Sharpshooters. When Captain Wheeler of the 2nd Battalion was wounded during the Battle of Gettysburg, Henry chose to remain with him as nurse, rather than retreat with his regiment. Both were taken as prisoners of war. Henry spent the next six months imprisoned in a Baltimore City jail at Point Lookout until his exchange. After returning to duty, he again was captured on April 9, 1865, just before the surrender of General Lee at Appomattox His worst injury was a bullet to the elbow that permanently locked his arm at a 90-degree angle. Despite this disability, he went on to become a successful surgeon. After the war, Henry continued his education, graduating from medical school at the University of Pennsylvania in 1867. Before starting his practice in 1869, he traveled abroad and studied at the University of Berlin, Prague, and Utrecht. In 1870, he married Adelaide de Schweinitz, who died within a year. On April 14, 1874, he married Emma Christine Fries (June 25, 1852–1945), the daughter of Francis Levin and Lisetta Maria Vogler Fries. The couple had six children. At the time of his death he was the surgeon for the Southern Railway and chief surgeon of the Winston-Salem Southbound Railway Company. He also held the position of president of the North Carolina Medical Society, the state board of health, and secretary of the state board of medical examiners. Ever reluctant to discuss his experiences of the war, Henry agreed to speak publicly to the citizens of Salem. He delivered his emotional story in the chapel of Salem Female Academy. The following are excerpts of his lecture:

> . . . I was detailed on picket duty . . . In front of me was an old field and scattered over it were dead men. Most of them were clad in their uniforms of blue or gray, perhaps a dozen were partly naked where their clothes had been stripped from unwounded parts of the body. They lay as they had fallen, some on their backs or faces, others twisted and contorted by their death struggle . . . How long I gazed

4] HENRY THEODORE BAHNSON   5] GEORGE ELIAS NISSEN

entranced I can not tell, but suddenly I heard footsteps. When I tried to move, my frozen clothing rattled and cracked, and with the first step I tumbled over. Crawling, and helped by my comrades, I managed to reach a fire, and there found Bryon Douthit who made me drink a quart or more of coffee, so hot that I could not taste anything for a week . . . We were paroled at Farmville, and begged food by the way, sometimes welcomed, often repulsed, and walked by slow stages on account of our weakness to Clover Station. Here we appropriated a construction train, and standing on a flat car rode to a burned bridge ten miles from Greensboro. Walking on, I reached home the second morning thereafter. I had been mourned for as dead. Some of my companies had taken the description given by a burying detail, of a young fellow resembling me, and marked his grave with a board on which they carved my name. My welcome home may be imagined. I had lost thirty eight pounds in the weeks since we left Petersburg, and was so emaciated and filthy that my father did not at first recognize me . . . To my mind come sad and grim and gloomy memories; the forms of my comrades and friends hurried to an untimely death by disease and wounds; left as prey to the birds of the air, and the beasts of the field, at best and unceremoniously shoveled into a shallow trench . . .

Henry died on January 16, 1917, in Forsyth County. (NCR.)

5] GEORGE ELIAS NISSEN

George Elias Nissen (September 27, 1839–September 19, 1913) was born to John Philip Nissen (1813–1874) and Mary Vawter. John began working as a wagon manufacturer at

6] NEWELL WESLEY SAPP   7] CAPT. RUFUS W. WHARTON

the age of 21. Five years before George was born, John bought a lot in Waughtown, North Carolina, erected a log cabin, and started his pioneer wagon shop. When North Carolina seceded, the Nissen Wagon Works was converted into a government workshop. Through powered machinery, wagons could be assembled faster and more economically. The Nissen Wagon Works supplied NC regiments with the essential wagons needed to transport supplies. On May 24, 1861, George volunteered with the 11th Regiment, NC Volunteers (which later became Co. E, 21st NC Infantry), at Salem. He was promoted to sergeant of Co. B, 1st Battalion, NC Sharpshooters, on April 26, 1862. After the war, he returned home to Winston, and he and his brother William managed the business under the name of the George E. Nissen Wagon Works. In one year the company produced up to 10,000 wagons. On December 20, 1866, George married Sarah "Sallie" Stafford and they had two children, Mary Estalla and Robert S. Nissen. (PCVM.)

6] NEWELL WESLEY SAPP

Newell Wesley Sapp enlisted on May 24, 1861, at age 24, with the Forsyth Grays, the 11th Regiment, NC Volunteers, which was organized in the township of Salem. Eventually this company became Co. E, 21st Regiment, NC Infantry. The next month, Newell was promoted to first sergeant. In April 1862, Companies E and B were detached from the 21st Regiment and re-organized into a new separate battalion consisting of two companies. This battalion was primarily known as the 1st NC Sharpshooters, but it was also known as the 9th Battalion, NC Infantry. Not only did these men engage in combat duty, they were also primary guards of the wagon trains, and were responsible for capturing deserters. At the close of the war, Newell held the rank of third lieutenant of Company B, 1st NC Sharpshooters. He returned to his home in Kernersville, where he resided until his death on July 30, 1904. He belonged to the United Confederate Veterans of the Norfleet Camp located in Winston-Salem. (RH.)

7] CAPT. RUFUS W. WHARTON

Capt. Rufus W. Wharton, a local Forsyth County attorney, commanded the 11th Regiment, NC Volunteers, the Forsyth Grays. This regiment was reorganized as Co. E, 21st Regiment, NC Infantry. The 1860 Forsyth County census listed Captain Wharton as being 32 years old with no family. Concerned for the well being of his troops, he wrote a letter to E.A. Vogler (the president of the Board of Sustenance of Forsyth County) requesting assistance for supplies:

> Camp Near Bunker Hill, Oct. 4th, 1862, E.A. Vogler, Esq. Dear Sir: Col. Hoke of the 21st NC Regiment and I have been consulting as to the best method of supplying our men with shoes and socks for the coming winter, and have concluded to appeal to the parents and friends of the soldiers to supply the articles, and we will send an officer to bring them to us. I therefore take the liberty of troubling you again. What we want is one pair of stout served shoes and two-pair of socks (woolen) for each man, and nothing else; other articles we can procure from the Government. Will you have an advertisement inserted in the "Sentinel" and "Press" asking the parents and friends of the members of Capt. Headley's Company to bring the above mentioned articles to some designated place in Salem by the 5th day of Nov. whence it will be brought to us by an officer sent for that purpose. You have done so much for us and still have so much on your hands, that I cannot ask you to attend to receiving and packing those articles, but probably some other public spirited citizen will undertake it. The same appeal will be made to the parents and friends of all the Companies in the Regiment and Battalion. I would be pleased to hear from you. Direct to Trimble's Brigade, Ewell's Division, Winchester, Va. Yours truly, R.W. Wharton.

8] JULIUS ROWLAND VOGLER

Julius Rowland Vogler (November 20, 1830–January 18, 1886) was born to Nathanael and Anna Maria (Fishel) Vogler. On May 24, 1861, he volunteered with the 11th Regiment, NC Volunteers (Co. E, 21st NC Infantry), in Salem. He was 30 years old. By September 1861, he had been promoted from first sergeant to captain, reporting to field and staff of this regiment. During this time he appointed Henry Bahnson as his assistant. Julius's military records report him as a member of Lewis's Brigade, Early's Division, 2nd Corps, Army of Northern Virginia. His records also show he was a member of Co. B, 1st Battalion NC Sharp Shooters, Trimble's Brigade. By the fall of 1864, he was attached to Gen. Jubal Early's division, and placed in charge of the commissary train. Julius wrote to his sister Maria about some of his hardships and news of local boys:

> Aug. 3, 1863, Camp New Orange C.H. Va. Dear Sister, Your kind letter was received a few days since, which was the first letter I received from home since I left Fredericksburg. You requested me to write more about the death of T. Lineback. He was with the wagons having been detailed as harness maker for the Brigade, when

8] Julius Rowland Vogler

9] William Masten

10] Edward R. Hull

11] John Madison and
Elizabeth Rebecca Frey Rothrock

our wagon train was attacked at Williamsport on Monday evening 6 July, he together with three teamsters & all extra men about the train took their muskets for the purpose of defending our train & ourselves, he was killed early in the action, a shell entirely separating one hip from his body & breaking the other leg, killing him instantly . . . In regard to Capt. Wheeler, he was badly wounded, his left arm was amputated half way between the hand & elbow, was also wounded in both thighs, the latter wounds are only flesh wounds. I left him on Saturday morning 4 July at the Brigade Hospital 4 miles from Gettysburg, he had recovered from the shock of amputation, was in good spirits & considered by the doctor to be doing well & in good condition . . . . Oct. 12, 1864, New Market Va. Dear Sister, . . . we attacked the enemy in front & flank simultaneously & completely routes [sic] him, capturing his entire contents, baggage of every description together with 1,500 prisoners . . . Among the casualities [sic] from our town are Maj. W.T. Pfoff [Pfohl] left wounded in Strasburg & I fear died soon after we left town. Lt. Foy wounded in left eye, Henry Voss Petticord of our county killed, the list has not yet been made out . . .

Julius R. Vogler survived the war and returned to his home in Salem. (HEV and PCVM.)

9] William Masten

William Masten volunteered for service with Co. D, 21st NC Infantry, when he was 21 years old. He was elected to first lieutenant on May 21, 1861, and he later served as the lieutenant of Co. A, 1st Battalion, NC Sharpshooters. William's niece, Polly Alice, wrote of him in her memoirs:

I was only a little over 3 years old when the war broke out . . . My mother's brother, Uncle William Masten, was one of the first volunteers from our section. He was a lieutenant and a very handsome young man. During the four years of struggle he would come home occasionally on furloughs. His last visit home is as vivid in my mind as if it were yesterday. It was shortly before the battle at Petersburg, Va. He stayed at our home as usual and on the morning when he set out to return to his regiment my mother filled his bag with all the good things to eat that she could get into it . . . Uncle William was killed at the battle of Petersburg. (SSD.)

10] Edward R. Hull

Edward R. Hull enlisted in Surry County on November 10, 1863. He joined Co. C, 21st NC Infantry, and was present or accounted for until his parole at Appomattox Court House on April 9, 1865. At the time of his enlistment, Edward left his wife, Sarah Dunnagan Hull, alone to care for their nine children: Will, Lydia, Ruben, twins Diane and Henry, Martha, Susan, Jane, and Lucinda. After Sarah's death, Hull married again, this time to Rhoda Seals. (HBJ.)

11] John Madison and Elizabeth Rebecca Frey Rothrock

John Madison Rothrock, the son of Solomon Rothrock and Anna Elisabeth (Nancy) Perryman, was born on September 30, 1840, at Friedberg, Stokes County. He volunteered for service on May 24, 1861, with Co. E, the Forsyth Grays, which came to be known as Co. E, 21st NC Infantry. He was present or accounted for until his transfer to Co. B, NC Regiment, 1st Battalion Sharpshooters. He served the entire war, sustaining no injuries. On May 28, 1865, upon returning home to Forsyth County, he married Elizabeth (Eliza) Rebecca Frey. In the 1870 Forsyth County Census, John is listed as a farmer, living with his wife and children: John F. (age four) and Mary A. (age two). (THR.)

12] Adrian L. Voss

Adrian L. Voss, along with many of the Salem boys, volunteered with the Forsyth Grays, Co. E, 21st NC Infantry, on May 24, 1861. On April 26, 1862, Co. E transferred to the 1st Battalion, NC Sharpshooters, and was redesignated as Co. B of that battalion. On July 14, 1861, Adrian traveled by rail to Richmond with his battalion to join the other Confederate regiments of the Army of Northern Virginia gathering at Manassas, Virginia. He fought bravely in the first Battle of Manassas. Amazingly, his regiment suffered no casualties, but the victory of the regiment was short-lived. Though no one was killed in the battle, many succumbed to disease. By September of 1862, almost 100 men in Adrian's regiment had lost their lives to typhoid. The outbreak was so quick and violent that Dr. Francis Shaffner from the 33rd Regiment was sent to help. He was successful in slowing the tide of the disease, but not quick enough to save Adrian, who died of typhoid fever on September 30, 1862. He was 21 years old. (RH.)

13] Dr. Matthew Rauley Banner

Dr. Matthew Rauley Banner was born on Mar. 8, 1827, in the township of Germanton. His parents were Joshua (1775–1846) and Martha "Patty" Bitting Banner (1782–1854), early pioneers of the Germanton area. On June 12, 1856, he married Miss A.B. Barrett of Charleston, TN, and they had five children. When the Civil War began, Matthew was enjoying a thriving dental practice and owned a large drugstore in Dalton, Georgia. He enlisted in the Confederate Army on Mar. 28, 1862. By the end of the war, he had attained the rank of lieutenant colonel. He participated in all the major battles in the East Tennessee area, and he fought in the Battle above the Clouds, Lookout Mountain, near Chattanooga. He was stationed at Vicksburg during the long siege and witnessed the fall of the city. After the war, he returned to Dalton, where he found his home and drugstore completely demolished. He moved his family to Banner Elk, North Carolina, in 1872 and built his home where Cannon-Memorial Hospital now stands. Matthew's wife organized the first Sunday school in Banner Elk and was influential in encouraging ministers to teach there. In 1880, the Banners moved to Jacksboro, Texas. The climate in that area relieved the frequent attacks of hemorrhaging he experienced from war wounds. The improvement in his health enabled Matthew to once again pursue his practice of dentistry. Mrs. Banner taught school for a period after moving to Jacksboro. (JSC.)

12] ADRIAN L. VOSS

13] DR. MATTHEW RAULEY BANNER

14] WILLIAM HILLARD AND NANCY LOVINIA FERGUSON HOLLAND

15] HENRY BENTON HAUSER

16] EDWARD JAMES BANNER

17] DR. JOHN FRANCIS AND CAROLINE LOUISA FRIES SHAFFNER

14] WILLIAM HILLARD AND NANCY LOVINIA FERGUSON HOLLAND

William Hillard Holland (1842–May 26, 1863) married Nancy Lovinia Ferguson, the daughter of John H. and Polly Kiser Ferguson, on October 18, 1861. When he enlisted with Co. C, 21st NC Infantry, on August 4, 1862, he was a 25-year-old resident of Stokes County. His commanders were Captains Bazillia Y. Graves, Byrd Snow, and Logan T. Whitlock. In May 1863, William was shot in the leg, which led to its amputation. Unfortunately, the surgery did not save Holland's life, and he died in the Richmond Hospital on May 26, 1863. (JBB.)

15] HENRY BENTON HAUSER

Henry Benton Hauser (September 14, 1834–July 15, 1913) was born in Stokes County to Demetrius (Timothy) and Maria Gertraut Hauser. On May 29, 1861, he volunteered for service in Stokes County with the Stokes County Mountain Boys, for a period of 12 months. His company later became Co. F, 21st NC Infantry. In 1862, Henry was promoted to sergeant. Captured at Fredericksburg on May 3, 1863, he was listed on the register of POWs at the Old Capitol Prison in Washington, D.C. On May 7, 1863, he was transferred to the prison in Fort Delaware, and was eventually exchanged for a Union POW. Upon his return, Henry was promoted to first lieutenant and transferred to the field and staff of the 21st Regiment. He was present or accounted for until his capture at Saylor's Creek, Virginia, on April 6, 1865. He again was confined at Old Capitol Prison until being transferred to Johnson's Island on April 19, 1865. He remained in prison until taking the Oath of Allegiance to the United States on June 18, 1865. During his service, Henry was wounded in the throat. He married Patience Emma Malinda Kirby and the couple had eight children. (SC.)

16] EDWARD JAMES BANNER

Edward James Banner (April 7, 1838–June 16, 1922) was born in Stokes County to Joshua David and Amy Weaver Ogburn Banner. Prior to the war, he made a living as a day laborer in Salem. On May 22, 1861, he volunteered for service with the 11th Regiment, NC Volunteers (Co. D., 21st NC Infantry). He was hospitalized on June 9, 1863, probably as a result of the Battle of Chancellorsville, and was furloughed to his home in Salem. About March 29, 1865, after his capture near Hatcher's Run, Edward deserted to the enemy. He signed the Oath of Allegiance to the Union, and was provided transportation to Hope, Indiana. On April 4, 1865, the Confederates listed him as a "Rebel Deserter." At the war's end, Edward returned to Stokes County. In 1892, he made news in the local newspaper. It seems that he and his father-in-law, Mr. Mat Ziglar, had a disagreement over a piece of land. Edward procured a double-barreled shotgun and emptied one of the barrels, "Scattering load all over Ziglar's face and body." Ziglar survived the wounds. Edward died at the age of 84 and is buried in the Oak Summit Methodist Cemetery in Forsyth County. (JSC.)

18] Byrd Snow

19] John Lewis Pratt

20] William Franklin Vogler

21] Ezekiel Wilmoth

17] Dr. John Francis and Caroline Louisa Fries Shaffner

In 1861, 22-year-old Dr. John Francis (Frank) Shaffner (1838–1908) volunteered with the 11th Regiment, NC Volunteers, commanded by Capt. A.H. Belo, a longtime friend of the Shaffner family. Because he had just graduated from Jefferson Medical College, Dr. Shaffner remained a private until he was commissioned as an assistant surgeon in the 33rd NC Infantry and the 4th NC Infantry. Later, he served as chief surgeon in Branch's and Ramseur's Brigade in the Army of Northern Virginia. He kept a day-by-day diary of his activities during the war, much of which has been preserved along with his personal letters. Many of his letters were to Caroline Louisa (Carrie) Fries (1839–1922), the daughter of Francis and Lisetta Vogler Fries. What began as a friendly correspondence with a longtime friend eventually resulted in a courtship. On February 3 and 4, 1865, Dr. Shaffner noted in his diary "twenty day furlough had been approved . . . Drew two months wages . . . Started my servant and horse home this morning." Dr. Shaffner and Miss Fries were married on February 16, 1865. (LS.)

18] Byrd Snow

Byrd Snow (1831–February 6, 1865) was born in Surry County to Dick and Sally Tucker Snow. In 1859, he married Mary B. Herring, the daughter of Hardin and Betsy Dudley Herring. They had two sons: Robert (b. 1861) and Bird L. (b. 1863). On May 20, 1861, at age 29, Byrd volunteered for service, joining the Blue Ridge Riflemen (later reorganized as Co. C., 21st Regiment, NC Infantry). During the months of April and May of 1862, he was promoted from private to first lieutenant, then to captain. During the Battle of Chancellorsville, he was wounded in the left arm, which had to be amputated. He remained on medical furlough until about November 1864. In February 1865, he lost his life at Hatcher's Run. In his later years, Maj. James Beall described Byrd's valor during the battle: "Hatcher's Run. It was here Captain Byrd Snow fell mortally wounded. He was in command of the regiment during his fight, as brave and true a soldier as ever drew sword in his country's honor." (HS.)

19] John Lewis Pratt

John Lewis Pratt was born in 1834 to William Gholson Pratt and Johanna Elizabeth Butner Pratt. He volunteered for service in the 11th Regiment, NC Volunteers, and on June 11, 1861, he was mustered in as a sergeant. On April 27, 1862, he was elected as first lieutenant of Co. K., 21st Regiment. On July 20, 1864, at Stephenson's Depot, Virginia, John was captured and confined to Camp Chase, Ohio. The following March, he received a parole and transferred for exchange to Boulware's and Cox's Wharves, James River, Virginia. (HY.)

20] William Franklin Vogler

William Franklin Vogler (April 11, 1843–November 24, 1901) was born to Gottlieb and Martha (Teague) Vogler. On May 22, 1861, within days of turning 18, he volunteered at

Salem as a private with the Forsyth Rifles, later organized as Co. D, 21st NC Infantry. He was present or accounted for through February 1865. He participated in some of the worst battles fought during the Civil War. As the regiment's teamster, he would occasionally ride between the horses on the wagon tongue for protection from enemy fire. On November 23, 1865, he married Mary-Elizabeth (Berrier) Spaugh. They made their home in the Vienna District of Winston, and later in East Bend, Yadkin County, and had four children: Glendora E., Rosa, Early Monroe, and Cora Lee. To support his family, William sold produce and drugs from his wagon, sometimes traveling as far as Pennsylvania and Georgia. From these same locations, he picked up much needed resources that were in demand in Yadkin and the surrounding counties. He died on November 24, 1901, and Mary died on October 27, 1908. They are both buried in the Moravian graveyard in Bethania. (BMV and PCVM.)

21] EZEKIEL WILMOTH

Ezekiel Wilmoth (c. 1833–July 1, 1863) was born in Surry County to Stephen Snow (1793–1861) and Elizabeth Snow Wilmoth (1798–1856). On October 27, 1852, he married Martha Sarah Hodges, the daughter of C. Hubbard and Mary Smith Hodges Sr. Ezekial and Martha had the following children: Bird, Lythia, and Elizabeth Wilmoth. Ezekiel volunteered in Surry County on May 20, 1861, and mustered in as private with the Blue Ridge Riflemen, which was later reorganized as Co. C, 21st NC Infantry. He received a promotion to musician (fifer) in November 1861. He was present or accounted for until July 1, 1863, when he was killed during the Battle of Gettysburg. His company was on the front line when the battle began. He is buried in the Gettysburg National Cemetery. (JSC.)

22] RILEY ROBERTSON BOYLES

Riley Robertson Boyles was born on August 3, 1846, in Stokes County to John William Boyles (July 31, 1809–April 11, 1887) and Charity Ferguson Boyles (March 26, 1809–August 8, 1898). Riley volunteered with the Co. I, 21st Regiment, NC Infantry, the Surry Marksmen. His company left Mount Airy on June 24, 1861, for Danville, and he was present or accounted for until his capture at Fort Stedman on March 25, 1865. He was confined to Point Lookout until his release on June 23, 1865, after signing the Oath of Allegiance. The Boyles family lost six sons to the Civil War (John Jr., Alexander M., Calvin H., James H., Augustine H., and Irvin E.); Riley was the only survivor. On June 9, 1867, he married Mary Catherine Newsom (May 12, 1853–March 21, 1931). They had 11 children. (JBB and TSB.)

23] COLEMAN BARNES ZIGLAR

Coleman Barnes Ziglar (March 18, 1818–October 23, 1899) was born in Stokes County to James Barbery and Susanna Zimmerman Ziglar. On Feb. 18, 1845, he married Priscella Ogburn, the daughter of Edmond and Elizabeth Williams Ogburn. Coleman enlisted in the Confederate Army at the age of 42 and on June 11, 1861, he was elected first lieutenant, Co.

22] Riley Robertson Boyles   23] Coleman Barnes Ziglar

K, 21st Regiment, NC Infantry. He later served as a private with Eli Holland's Company, 7th Regiment, NC Sr. Reserves. He died on October 23, 1899, at the age of 81; Priscella died on December 10, 1915, at the age of 90. They are both buried at Matthews Chapel Church of Christ in Winston-Salem. (ST.)

24] Allen William Bevel

Allen William Bevel (September 6, 1834–May 21, 1899) made his living as a carpenter and blacksmith prior to his enlistment. He volunteered on June 11, 1861, with Co. D, 21st Regiment., NC Infantry. Sometime after the war, Allen brought a noble cannon to Winston-Salem from eastern North Carolina. He first placed it on the land where the Benton Convention Center now stands. About 1890, he moved the cannon to Kester Mill Road, where it remained in a rock quarry until Troy Church traded a single-barrel shotgun and $10 for the cannon barrel. The lumber for the tail stock of the carriage came from Shaffner's farm, now known as Sherwood Forest. With the assistance of a blacksmith, Troy made black irons for the cannon. By 1961, he had finished the carriage and the cannon fired once again at Civil War re-enactment sites. (TC.)

25] Edwin Theophilus Hauser

Edwin Theophilus Hauser was probably born in Yadkin County and was a farmer by trade. He joined the Confederate Army in Yadkin County on May 21, 1861, enlisting with Co. B,

21st NC Infantry, under Capt. John K. Connelly. Edwin mustered in as a sergeant. On February 1, 1862, at the age of 21, he received a disability discharge.

26] OFFICERS OF THE 21ST REGIMENT

During the months of May-June 1861, the North Carolina State Government sent two representatives to recruit 12 companies of infantry for service in the northern Piedmont. After each company was recruited and officers elected, they were ordered to Danville, Virginia, in June. These companies mustered into Confederate service as the 11th Regiment, NC Volunteers. On November 14, 1861, the Volunteers were redesignated as the 21st Infantry Regiment, NC Troops, with soldiers from Davidson, Yadkin, Surry, Forsyth, Stokes, Rockingham, and Guilford Counties. Co. B and E of the 21st Infantry were reorganized as the 1st Regiment, NC Infantry Battalion Sharpshooters. They engaged in 19 battles and were present during the surrender at Appomattox Court House on April 9, 1865. The following officers of the 21st Regiment are in the left image: (lower left) Capt. Rueben Everett Wilson, Co. B; (lower right) Sec. Lt. Louis Edward, Co. A; (middle) Col. Robert F. Hoke; (top left) Capt. Rufus Watson Wharton; (top right) Capt. John K. Conally, Co. B. The right image portrays the following officers: (bottom) Frst. Lt. and Adjutant William Graves Foy; (lower left) Maj. W.J. Pfohl; (lower right) Maj. James F. Beall; (middle) Col. William Whedbee Kirkland; (top) Col. Saunders Fulton; (top left) Lt. Col. B.Y. Graves; (top right) Lt. Col. Alexander Miller. (NCR.)

27] ALFRED HORATIO BELO

Alfred Horatio Belo (May 27, 1839–April 19, 1901) was born in Salem. His father, Edward Belo, was a wealthy merchant who was one of the founders of the Wachovia National Bank in Winston and the Roanoke and Southern Railroad. When the Civil War broke out, Alfred volunteered for active service in the Confederate Army, and was elected captain of 11th Regiment, NC Volunteers. Later, he served as lieutenant colonel of the 55th Regiment, NC Infantry. Alfred served during the Virginia Campaigns. He sustained injuries at Gettysburg in 1863, as well as at Cold Harbor during Grant's fierce assault on the Confederate lines. By the end of the war, he had attained the rank of colonel. He was also present with General Lee during the surrender at Appomattox. After the war, Alfred decided to seek a new start in the southwest. After a short visit to Salem, he traveled by horse to Texas. He signed his Oath of Allegiance while in Dallas in April 1865. In August 1865, he began working for the *Galveston News*. On June 30, 1868, he married Miss Cornelius Ennis in Galveston, Texas. The couple had two children, Alfred Jr. and Jeanette. Alfred purchased the *Galveston News* in 1875. In 1881, he formed a stock company, authorized by its charter to publish newspapers at Galveston and such other points in the state of Texas as they might select. He duplicated the *News* and issued it simultaneously at Galveston and Dallas. Each paper had its own local department, the same editorial writers, the same branch offices in New York, Washington, Chicago, and elsewhere, and the same press service throughout Texas. The matter consolidated at either Galveston or Dallas, according to convenience, then transmitted by telegraph from one office to the other, 315 miles away. Colonel Belo eventually returned to his native state of North Carolina and died in Asheville. Today, BELO, Inc., is one of the nation's largest media companies, with 1998 revenues exceeding $1.4 billion. BELO owns and operates a diversified group of television

24] ALLEN WILLIAM BEVEL

25] EDWIN THEOPHILUS HAUSER

26] OFFICERS OF THE 21ST REGIMENT

broadcasting, newspaper publishing, cable news, and interactive media assets in 22 markets throughout the nation. (CVM.)

28] WILLIAM J. PFOHL

William J. Pfohl was one of the first citizens of Salem to volunteer with the Forsyth Rifles, Co. D, 21st Regiment, NC Infantry. Initially assigned as the company's orderly sergeant, Pfohl eventually attained the rank of major. He was present or accounted for throughout the war until his death at Strasburg, Virginia. In his 1901 monograph, Maj. James Beall described Pfohl's death during the Battle of Fisher's Hill:

> General Ramseur was seen to fall, and Johnson [Pvt. Johnson, ambulance driver] was ordered by Major Pfohl to go after him, which he did under a terrific fire. He succeeded in getting him, but was overtaken and captured on the retreat. General Pegram seeing that the day was lost to the Confederates, ordered the division to fall back, saying: 'Men, you must do this in order—firing as you retreat, for your own and the army's safety demand it.' Never was greater heroism displayed by both men and officers than in this terrible retreat. Then the enemy, maddened by recent defeat, and flushed with sudden victory, with their whole line made a furious assault upon our discomfited line, which was driven back in great confusion. In our futile efforts to stem the tide of battle that threatened to overwhelm us, we lost many brave officers and men. Among the killed was the heroic Pfohl, commander of the regiment. No man ever exhibited in such a time greater coolness, skill and bravery, which excited the admiration of his men. (NCR.)

29] SPRUCE MCKAUGHAN AND DRUSILLA SWAIM PEDICORD

Spruce McKaughan Pedicord was born on February 1, 1824, in Stokes County to Keelon and Grizella Ledford Pedicord. On March 28, 1862, at the age of 35, he enlisted with Co. D, 21st Regiment, NC Infantry. He was present or accounted for until his discharge in August 1862, by reason of age. Long before the war, he married Drusilla Swaim (b. March 23, 1827), also of Stokes County, the daughter of Jonathan Swaim and Eva Snow. According to the 1860 Forsyth County Census, Spruce was living in the Broadbay District of Forsyth County with his wife and four children. In the 1870 census, he and his family were residents of Yadkin County. Spruce and Drusilla eventually had six children: William M., Hamilton Addison, John H., Andrew Jackson, Alexander R., and Lewis. (MHB.)

30] SAUNDERS FULTON

Saunders Fulton volunteered with Co. G, 21st Regiment, NC Infantry, which was organized in Germanton, Stokes County, on May 30, 1861. He served the Confederate Army as a major, lieutenant colonel, and colonel, and his regiment participated in the majority of the battles that took place in northern Virginia. After the Battle of Winchester in May of 1862,

27] ALFRED HORATIO BELO   28 WILLIAM J. PFOHL

29] SPRUCE MCKAUGHAN AND DRUSILLA SWAIM PEDICORD

General Trimble complimented him and his regiment for their gallant conduct. Saunders was killed in August 1862, during the Second Battle of Manassas. He was eulogized as a man who "was absolutely without fear, and who evidently believed he was not to be killed in battle." (NCR.)

31] BAZILLA YANCY GRAVES

Bazilla Yancy Graves was born in Surry County in 1835 to Judge Solomon and Mary Franklin Graves. On May 20, 1861, he volunteered with the Blue Ridge Riflemen, later reorganized as Co. C, 21st NC Infantry. That same day he was elected to serve as their captain. After two years of service, he received a promotion to major, reporting to field and staff. During the Second Battle of Manassas, he received wounds so serious he was no longer able to serve the Confederacy. His first wife was Mattie Rankin. In 1876 he married again, this time to Mary Moore of Stokes County. They had two sons: William and Bazilla Yancy Jr., who married Virginia Bitting. (NCR.)

32] WILLIAM WHEDBEE KIRKLAND

By the time the Civil War started, William Whedbee Kirkland had a reputation and the experience of a professional soldier. On July 3, 1861, he was elected the first colonel of the 21st NC Troops. In his career, he served under the command of Colonel Early and Generals Trimble, Hoke, and Ewell. He fought in many of the major battles of the war. During the Battle of Gettysburg, while waving his sword and cheering on his men, William was shot through the thigh, but did not leave the field. After this battle, he was promoted to brigadier general. On September 7, 1863, he assumed the command of General Pettigrew's old brigade of Heth's Division, A.P. Hill's corps, consisting of the 11th, 26th, 44th, 47th, and 52nd NC Regiments. His military leadership was of the highest order and respect. He was in Greensboro when General Lee surrendered. (NCR.)

33] ALEXANDER MILLER

Alexander Miller was 28 when he volunteered with the Forsyth Rifles. After the company reached Danville, Virginia, he was appointed third lieutenant of Co. D, 21st Regiment, NC Infantry. He continued to receive promotions throughout the war. Just a few days after he left Winston with his company, his father died. His mother, widowed and with two sons in the war, was left to care for herself and assume full responsibility as proprietor of "Miller's Hotel." In July 1863, Alexander was severely wounded during the Battle of Gettysburg after he picked up a fallen battle flag and held it high amid the deafening roar of the cannons. He was hospitalized and eventually died on August 2, 1863. His remains were sent home to Winston, and he is buried in Woodlawn Cemetery next to his brother, Frst. Lt. John Miller, who also died in the war. (NCR.)

30] SAUNDERS FULTON

31] BAZILLA YANCY GRAVES

32] WILLIAM WHEDBEE KIRKLAND

33] ALEXANDER MILLER

34] WILLIAM GRAVES FOY

35] JOHN W. MILLER

36] JOHN HENRY
HAUSER

37] OFFICERS OF THE
21ST REGIMENT

38] LOGAN T.
WHITLOCK

34] WILLIAM GRAVES FOY

William Graves Foy was born in 1845 in Surry County to Miles and Sebena Foy. On May 24, 1861, at the age of 16, he traveled to the neighboring county of Forsyth and volunteered for service with the 11th Regiment NC Volunteers (Co. E, 21st Regiment, NC Infantry). In January 1862, after his promotion to sergeant, William transferred to Company C, and in June 1863 he was promoted to second lieutenant. He fought valiantly at Gettysburg, gaining him another promotion to first lieutenant. He then transferred to field and staff. He sustained serious injuries to his left eye and nose during the Battle of Fisher's Hill. He remained on the official records as absent-wounded until he retired to the Invalid Corp on March 3, 1865. (NCR.)

35] JOHN W. MILLER

In the early 1860s, John W. Miller (April 19, 1842–May 4, 1863) lived with his parents, Harmon and Elender Miller, his older brother Alexander, and his two younger sisters, Ellen and Sallie. When the call for duty came in May 1861, John was the first to volunteer with the 11th Regiment, NC Volunteers, later reorganized as Co. B, 21st Regiment, NC Infantry. In 1863, he lost his life during the Battle of Marye's Heights, near Fredericksburg. His obituary describes his valor:

> First Lt. John W. Miller of Co. B, 21st NC Regiment and the brother of Maj. Alex. Miller, [died] May 4, 1863, at the recapture of Marye's Heights, near Fredricksburg, Virginia. He was the first who registered his name as a volunteer in Forsyth County, and nobly filled the position of an officer and soldier. He passed unscathed through all the battles of Manassas, when, after men had fallen while holding the battle-flag, he grasped it and, waving it in one hand and his sword in the other, he was struck with a minnie ball, which caused a severe wound in his hand. Receiving furlough, he came home but returned again to the army before his wound was entirely healed. The remains of Lt. Miller were interred in Woodland Cemetery [in Winston-Salem]. (NCR.)

36] JOHN HENRY HAUSER

John Henry Hauser (1847–1930) volunteered for service with the Yadkin Gray Eagles, who came to be known as Co. B, 21st NC Infantry, on May 12, 1861. He was present or accounted for through October 1861, and may have served with the 1st Battalion, NC Sharpshooters.

37] OFFICERS OF THE 21ST REGIMENT

Officers of the 21st Regiment pose for a photograph. They are as follows: (bottom) Capt. J.O. Blackburn, Co. G; (lower left) Sgt. James Daniel McIver, Co. A; (lower right) Capt. John

W. Miller, Co. D; (middle) Capt. Samuel C. James, Co. D; (top) Capt. J.H. Miller, Co. A; (top left) Frst. Lt. Logan T. Whitlock, Co. C; (top right) Capt. John Eli Gilmer, Co. M. The 21st Regiment was engaged in the bloodiest battles of the war—some researchers document these battles as being some of the greatest in history. The first major engagement of the 21st Regiment was in Manasass, at the center of the Confederate line of battle. (NCR.)

38] Logan T. Whitlock

Logan T. Whitlock was born in Surry County to Charles and Celia Roberts Whitlock. He volunteered for service on May 20, 1861, with Co. C, 21st NC Infantry, which was organized in Mount Airy, Surry County. He was chosen to serve his company as second lieutenant on the day of his enlistment. One year later, he was promoted to first lieutenant. In June of 1862, during a battle at Cross Keys, Virginia, he sustained his first battle wounds. He was relieved of duty until March 1, 1863. In March 1865, he was promoted to captain. One month later he was taken prisoner during the Battle of Sayler's Creek, Virginia. He was imprisoned at Johnson's Island, Ohio, on April 21, 1865, and remained there until taking the Oath of Allegiance on June 20, 1865. (HBJ.)

Seven

BATTLEFIELDS AND PRISONS:
THEIR SPIRITS CALL TO US

A LARGE UNION WAGON PARK was photographed in May 1864 by Timothy H. O'Sullivan in the vicinity of Brandy Station, Virginia. The Battle of Brandy Station took place on June 9, 1863. Approximately 19,000 mounted men were involved in this cavalry battle (22,000 soldiers were involved overall). It has been written that, for the first time in the Civil War, the Union cavalry matched the Confederate horsemen in skill and determination. Over 1,000 men lost their lives. (LOC.)

THIS PONTOON BRIDGE CROSSING THE JAMES RIVER, VIRGINIA, during Grant's Wilderness Campaign was photographed by James B. Gardner. (LOC.)

THE RUINS OF A DEPOT destroyed when Sherman departed Atlanta were photographed in 1864 by George N. Barnard (1819–1902). After raiding Rebel supply lines, Judson Kilpatrick assaulted the Atlanta West Point Railroad on the evening of August 18, 1864. The following day, Kilpatrick's men attacked the Jonesborough supply depot on the Macon & Western Railroad. Their plans of destruction had intensified by the time they reached Lovejoy's Station on the 20th, resulting in great amounts of supplies being destroyed. The track at Lovejoy's Station was rebuilt and was back in operation in two days. (LOC.)

THESE UNION GRAVES AT CEDAR MOUNTAIN, VIRGINIA, mark casualties from the Second Battle of Bull Run. The image was taken and published by photographer Timothy H. O'Sullivan (1840–1882) in August 1862. (LOC.)

THESE CONFEDERATE FORTIFICATIONS IN YORKTOWN, VIRGINIA, were reinforced with bales of cotton. This photograph from the Peninsula Campaign (May-August 1862) in the main eastern theater of war was taken and published in June 1862. (LOC.)

AFRICAN-AMERICAN SOLDIERS collect the bones of soldiers killed in the Battle of Cold Harbor, Virgina, May 31–June 12, 1864. Sixty-two thousand Confederate soldiers and 108,000 Union Soldiers assembled for battle. The principal commanders were Lt. Gen. Ulysses S. Grant, Maj. Gen. George G. Meade, and Gen. Robert E. Lee. Of the 15,500 estimated casualties, only 2,500 were Confederate soldiers. Photographer John Reekie took this image in April 1865. (LOC.)

THE TEMPORARY MARKER OF GEN. J.E.B. STUART in Hollywood Cemetery, Richmond, VA, is shown here in a photograph created and published in 1865. (LOC.)

AFRICAN-AMERICAN TEAMSTERS pose c. 1864 near the signal tower in Bermuda Hundred, Virginia. The following letter to Lt. Gen. Grant was written by Maj. Gen. Butler concerning the use of colored troops:

HEADQUARTERS Oct. 3, 1864—11:30 a.m. Lieutenant-General GRANT: All quiet during the night, an attempt was made on Kautz's and Birney's pickets, on the Darbytown and New Market roads, last evening, which was easily repulsed, and by Birney with the capture of seventeen prisoners. Lieutenant Michie is at work on the new line with 1,000 colored troops. Will you telegraph to the secretary of War for a brevet major for Michie in his corps? I wish him as my chief engineer. If gallant, unwearied, and most meritorious services are ever deserving they are in this case. Also, an order that he be put on duty in his brevet rank. I have set Ludlow's extra men at Dutch Gap at work on the redoubt on signal Hill near him. Four regiments of Pickett's division are over here from the Bermuda line between Appomattox and James, leaving about 2,500 men there. I believe I could break through on the left with 3,000 negroes. Can we not have the other corps here? B.F. BUTLER, Major-General, Commanding. (LOC.)

PHOTOGRAPHER TIMOTHY O'SULLIVAN documented the strength of the works and the effects of the bombardment on the "Pulpit" of Fort Fisher, North Carolina, in January 1865. On January 15 of that year, Fort Fisher and Wilmington, North Carolina, the last resort of the blockade-runners, were sealed off by Admiral David D. Porter's squadron of nearly 60 warships and the U.S. Colored Troops of Paine's Division. It was a Union victory with a cost of about 2,000 lives. This image is one of a number belonging to the Federal Navy regarding seaborne expeditions against the Atlantic Coast of the Confederacy. (LOC.)

THE BATTLE OF DREWRY'S BLUFF was fought May 12–16, 1864. Under the command of Gen. P.G.T. Beauregard, 18,000 Confederate soldiers were assembled to confront the 30,000 Union soldiers under the command of Maj. Gen. Benjamin Butler. Soundly thrashed by the Confederates, Butler withdrew his troops. The battle stopped Butler's offensive against Richmond, Virginia. This 1865 image shows the interior of Fort Darling (Confederate), at Drewry's Bluff, Virginia, on the James River. (LOC.)

THIS CAPTURED CONFEDERATE ENCAMPMENT was located near Petersburg, Virginia. After the Confederate defeat at Five Forks on April 1, 1865, Grant and Meade ordered a general assault against the Petersburg. That evening, Lee ordered the evacuation of Petersburg and Richmond. Grant had achieved one of the major military objectives of the war: the capture of Petersburg, which led to the fall of Richmond, the capital of the Confederacy. The estimated casualties of this battle included 7,750 dead; of that total, 4,250 were Confederate soldiers. Hundreds of others were captured. (LOC.)

FEDERAL SOLDIERS stand in front of the bomb-proof Fort Burnham (the former Confederate Fort Harrison) in Virginia.

THE PRINCIPAL FORT IN CENTREVILLE, VIRGINIA, was photographed by George N. Barnard (1819–1902) in March 1862. (LOC.)

FALLS CHURCH, VIRGINIA, also referred to as "The Church," served as the Confederate winter quarters during 1861–62. It is shown here between 1860 and 1865. (LOC.)

FEDERAL SOLDIERS rebuilt the Orange & Alexandria Railroad bridge over Cedar Run in the vicinity of Catlett's Station, Virginia, in 1863. (LOC.)

LOOKOUT MOUNTAIN is visible in the background of this March 1862 photograph of a U.S. military train at a depot in Chattanooga. On November 23–24, 1863, Union forces captured Orchard Knob and Lookout Mountain. The next day, what seemed to be an impregnable Confederate position on Missionary Ridge was penetrated. The Federals held Chattanooga, the "Gateway to the Lower South," which eventually supplied and supported Sherman's 1864 Atlanta Campaign. (LOC.)

THE "KEEPERS OF PT. LOOKOUT, MARYLAND" were Brig. Gen. James Barnes and his staff, who commanded the district of St. Mary's during the latter part of the war. Pt. Lookout was the largest prison in the north. In all, over 50,000 men, both military and civilian, were held prisoner here.

THE STEAMER *NEW YORK* waits at Aiken's Landing, Virginia, during the war for an exchange of prisoners. (LOC.)

A GROUP OF CONFEDERATES captured at Cedar Mountain are shown here on the balcony of the Culpeper Court House, Virginia, shortly after the Second Battle of Bull Run in July-August 1862. In early August, Maj. Gen. John Pope led his forces south into Culpeper County with the objective of capturing the rail junction at Gordonsville. A Confederate counterattack led by A.P. Hill successfully repressed the Federals. Over a thousand men were lost on each side. (LOC.)

CONFEDERATE PRISONERS were photographed in 1864 at a railroad depot in Chattanooga. The image is related to the Battle of Chattanooga, September-October 1863. On October 17, Maj. Gen. Ulysses S. Grant received command of the Western armies. Maj. Gen. William T. Sherman soon established a new supply line with his four divisions. Realizing the importance of capturing the Confederate rail, the Federals began their offensive operations in mid-November. (LOC.)

DURING THE BATTLE OF GETTYSBURG, Gen. Robert E. Lee's headquarters was located on the Chambersburg Pike. The cemetery gatehouse is shown at left. All three images were taken in 1863, the year of that fateful battle. (Image of headquarters and gatehouse LOC.)

After Four Years of Battle, approximately 630,000 deaths, and over 1 million casualties, Gen. Robert E. Lee succumbed to the inevitable. He surrendered the Confederate Army of Northern Virginia to Lt. Gen. Ulysses S. Grant at the home of Wilmer and Virginia McLean in the town of Appomattox Court House, Virginia, on Palm Sunday, April 9, 1865. After the surrender, Federal soldiers all but ransacked the McLean's home. Furniture and personal items, including the doll of McLean's seven-year-old daughter Lula, were taken by the Federal soldiers as souvenirs. One of these soldiers was Capt. Robert Todd Lincoln, son of the president of the United States. After the surrender, 27,805 Confederate soldiers were paroled. (LOC.)

The following poem was written in a Bible owned by Alpha Cook, Co. A, 21st Regiment, NC Troops, Hoke's Brigade, Early's Division. Alpha resided in Clemmons, North Carolina, and was killed in the Battle of Cedar Creek in 1864. His Bible was taken from his corpse by a Union soldier on the battlefield and eventually returned to his mother 15 years later. Alpha Cook was the son of Jacob and Nancy Rebecca Jarvis Cook of Clemmons, North Carolina. (FJM/LOC)

I want to see my Mother nigh, Oh can you call her here?
It wouldn't seem so hard to die to have my Mother near.
My home is in the mountains, up where the pine trees wave;
Was there I heard the bugle calling for the brave.
"But, I want to see my Mother, her tender, Loving eye--
and hear her footstep, to hear her call my name.
To have her pray beside me--No other prays the same.
"I want to clasp her dear hand, and hold her to my heart,,
And say, "God bless you Mother," once more before we part.
Mother, Mother, come to me! I cannot die alone.
Come quick my Angel Mother, Oh, Don't you hear me groan..
"Oh No, she doesn't hear me, she doesn't know my pain
and She'll never, ever, see me in my old seat again
She's tending darling sister--I've dreamed of her all day.
And I hear my little prattler lisping, "Brudder far away."
"Oh God! O Chaplain, Hear Me! Pray Heaven will give me grace;
to still this Dying longing To see my Mother's face.
There. Peace! I'll turn to Jesus, He Never would complain-
He came to save his country Yet Jesus too was slain.
Yes, Brother, God has heard you, He's calmed my agony.
My sins are all forgiven now: and he is all to me.
Then Tell my blessed Mother, I'm dying peacefully-
Christ Jesus now is Mother! and He'll take care of me.